I have enjoyed several Semester at Sea voyages with Lloyd on the *S.S. Universe* and greatly admired his ability to deal with hundreds of students, while at the same time coping with all the innumerable emergencies that arise at sea (tidal waves, mutinies, pirates, sea serpents, etc., etc.). I wish him all success with his future endeavours and hope he will come sailing into Colombo harbour again one day.

— *Sir Arthur C. Clarke, Author*

శ

Lloyd Lewan has been my mentor for over seventeen years and has been the single greatest influence in my leadership development. He taught me the power of vision and influence and the need to lead from both my head and my heart. He fuels and fans the flame of my passion for the art of leadership.

— *Terry Anderson, Director, Lewan & Associates, Inc.*

Lloyd Lewan is the best kept secret in Denver. His influence and gentle hand have led and guided so many lives, but you would hardly notice. This is real leadership.

— *Cinthia Andrews, President,*
The Zach Foundation for Burned Children

I have had the pleasure of knowing Lloyd Lewan for the past ten years. During this time, I have observed a true master of leadership at work. With his honest, humble, and knowledgeable outlook on life, he has enlightened my life personally and professionally. He has truly mastered leadership in all aspects.

— *Thomas G. Austin, Vice President, UBS/PaineWebber*

Lloyd Lewan has proven to be a dedicated community leader in many arenas: a successful businessman, an invaluable advocate for the Zach Foundation for Burned Children, a teacher and proponent of life-long learning, and a tireless champion to those who are less fortunate in our community. Lloyd is a stellar example of all that can be accomplished with the energy, dedication, and enthusiasm inherent in those who choose to lead.

— Ray Barnes, former Fire Chief, Aurora, Colorado

Lloyd Lewan knows that a leader must show respect, act consistently, and inspire others with a vision of possibility. He is a true world leader, having met with people as diverse as heads of state to street children. Whoever it may be, Lloyd generates respect by consistently granting it to others.

— Dr. Kirk Bergstrom, President & CEO, WorldLink Media

On two separate Semester at Sea voyages, I had the distinct privilege of watching Dr. Lloyd Lewan practice sound leadership by motivating a diverse group of students, faculty, and staff on a ship sailing around the world.

— Dr. Michael Bikerman, Professor Emeritus,
University of Pittsburgh

Dr. Lloyd Lewan has enriched the lives of thousands of people for many years by practicing leadership at the highest levels of idealism and commitment. At last we have a chance to directly benefit from his wisdom and years of experience by reading his wonderful new book, *to be a LEADER.*

— Dr. Ron Billingsley, University of Colorado

Over the years I've had the privilege of knowing many great leaders in the political arena, the marketplace, and the church. Lloyd may have the greatest insight into what leadership is all about of anyone I've ever been privileged to know. His understanding of people, his care for them, and his ability to lead them is unique.

— Dr. Mark A. Brewer, Senior Pastor,
Bel Air Presbyterian Church, Los Angeles

Lloyd's leadership ideas and strategies are never more relevant than in today's world. Every business owner and aspiring leader will find a wealth of practical wisdom in this book that is applicable to real world situations. Lloyd was instrumental in my success, and I highly recommend these teachings for those who want to make a difference in their organization and in the lives of their people.

— Fred Cannataro, President, Lewan & Associates, Inc.

Lloyd Lewan is genuine and authentic. His passion and belief in real leadership have been exemplified in his commitment to practice leadership and in his devotion to education. He has been a role model and mentor and has had tremendous influence in my personal and professional growth.

— Ben Chao, Anthem, Inc.
West Region, Executive Director, IT

Lloyd Lewan was not only the most popular teacher at Chapman that I have come to know, but also he was one of the most effective. Many years after he left Chapman, I invited Lloyd to present our annual commencement address. The response to this address, not surprising knowing Lloyd, was electrifying. His theme, which focused on leadership and the differing skill sets relating to leadership and management, hit a very responsive chord. In the countless commencement addresses I have heard, no speaker was able to reach the hearts and the minds of our graduates as Lloyd was able to do. People are still talking about it five years later!

— Dr. Jim Doti, President, Chapman University

Lloyd Lewan combines knowledge, compassion, insight, and instinct to provide a leadership style that inspires young and old alike. He provides methods for everyone that show them how to find that spark within to achieve at even greater levels.

— Norm Early, former District Attorney, Denver, Colorado

Lloyd Lewan is one of the greatest men I know. His years of honest service, dedication, and leadership have given him an extraordinary insight and understanding of people. His passion and acceptance of humanity is seen through his compassionate love for people, whether they are on top or whether they are on the bottom. Lloyd's capacity to go the distance with people is unparalleled. God reserves the very best for us who leave the timing to Him. It is at this time that God has give us the very best in Lloyd and in his writings.

—Randy Gradishar, former All-Pro Denver Bronco,
Leadership Manager, Phil Long Ford Dealerships

Among the qualities of leadership that Lloyd Lewan demonstrates are diligence, imagination, and vision. Having served with him as part of his faculty and staff on four Semester at Sea voyages, we have been inspired by his work ethic and idealism and have been privileged to follow his lead in promoting international awareness and understanding.

— Dr. William J. Griswold, Professor Emeritus;
Jean S. Griswold, Office of International Programs, retired,
Colorado State University

Lloyd Lewan doesn't just talk about leadership; he lives it — in his community, in his family, in his business, in his industry, and in his world. He is always reaching out and bringing others along — students, women, people who are struggling. He is a great friend and inspiration to so very many of us.

— Barbara Grogan, President & CEO,
Western Industrial Contractors, Inc.

What does it take to be a leader? That answer is embodied in the spirit, qualities, and commitment of Lloyd Lewan. His record of successful leadership in business, education, philanthropy, and community service is legendary. The wisdom and insight he shares will be instructive as he "charts the course" for others to follow.

— Dr. Dorothy Horrell, Executive Director,
Bonfils-Stanton Foundation

To know leadership is to know Lloyd Lewan. Over the years I have observed and learned much from this man. He allowed me and encouraged me to develop my skills in working with many different types of people in many walks of life. Lloyd's experiences with people around the world have created a man who is true to the human spirit. As I interact with young people who have made bad choices, I am constantly reminded of the many conversations that Lloyd and I have had relating to the human condition. We have said over and over that we do not condone their acts and choices, but we do value their lives. From the hours waiting in the hospital for the birth of my children to the murder of my nephew, Lloyd has been by my side providing me with leadership, support, and love.

— *Reverend Leon Kelly, Executive Director,*
Open Door Youth Gang Alternatives

I thoroughly enjoyed watching Lloyd Lewan's exceptional leadership skill during a Semester at Sea voyage. He has a special gift with young people.

— *Richard Lamm, Director, Center for Public Policy*
and Contemporary Issues, University of Denver,
former Governor of Colorado, 1975-1987

Having sailed with Dr. Lewan on two voyages, I have learned more about leadership from him than from any business course I have taken. His philosophy combines the best of the task orientation of management with the inspiration of leadership.

— *Michael L. Peralta, Director, Strategic Partnerships,*
Advertising.com

Lloyd Lewan has practiced and taught leadership successfully in the competitive business environment and higher education. This rare combination of experiences gives him the insight, the credibility, and the passion to show audiences how they can become more effective leaders by becoming better human beings.

— *Dr. Eric E. Reno, President, Red Rocks College*

As a friend and business advisor for more than fifteen years, I have witnessed first hand Lloyd's uncanny insight into the meaning of leadership by force of character and influence as opposed to office or position. Servant leadership is made clear.

— *Thomas N. Scheffel, Attorney at Law,*
Scheffel & Associates, P.C.

Lloyd Lewan is a leader who combines enthusiasm, extraordinary sensitivity, and a genuine caring for others. He encourages others to take responsibility for their actions and to become leaders themselves. He is a leader among leaders. Throughout his career, he has opened a door to the world for so many; and, in so doing, he has changed their lives forever. We, as faculty members (Fall 2000 Sail) and as people, learned so much from this remarkable man.

— *Dr. Stephen Sloan, Professor of Political Science,*
University of Oklahoma;
Dr. Roberta Sloan, Professor of Theater,
University of Central Oklahoma

Lloyd Lewan is a consumate leader. Motivating in the community, among his business associates, and with those who through his inspiration will lead some day, he is a leader by example. His message comes from the heart with conviction and strength. All who cross his path walk away better people, for Lloyd believes that good leaders need to be good people. He is the example of leadership in living color.

— *Kevin Smith, Colorado Vice President,*
Qwest Communications

Lloyd Lewan's gift of leadership is the product of strength blended with grace. Lloyd leads with a strength of purpose and enduring energy, which inspires others to join him. But, it is his grace that truly sets him apart. Lloyd Lewan teaches and encourages others to lead, and he revels in the success of his allies. He is the leader's leader.

— *Keith D. Tooley, Attorney at Law,*
Welborn Sullivan Meck & Tooley, P.C.

Lloyd Lewan has been a friend, a colleague, and a mentor for more than twenty-five years. I marveled at his leadership skills and benefited immensely as I watched him during the many times he faced a crisis. Over these many years, I have carried with me the important advice he gave me on our only voyage together. He emphasized in our many meetings: "It is not what you do but how you do it that counts." His advice has been important to me in my many years of shipboard education.

— *Dr. John Tymitz, Chief Executive Officer,*
Institute for Shipboard Education, Semester at Sea,
University of Pittsburgh

Lloyd embodies the rare traits of outstanding leader and good friend. During our voyage together, he expressed a genuine interest in each student's potential with a great degree of trust. This trust was answered with an uncommon loyalty, which reflects on Lloyd's leadership and general faith in humanity. I believe that I speak for every student on board when I say that I would follow Lloyd anywhere.

> — *Nick Wells, Student, Semester at Sea, Fall 2000*

I sailed with Lloyd after having ten years of experience in student affairs. I was amazed by the wealth of knowledge I gained during the one hundred days on Semester at Sea with him. It surpassed any other previous professional development in my career. He is an amazing leader, mentor, and student-affairs practitioner!

> — *Cindy Zomcheck, Colorado College*

to be a
LEADER

LEADERSHIP BEYOND
MANAGEMENT

Lloyd S. Lewan

RP

Remington Press
Denver, Colorado

to be a LEADER: Leadership Beyond Management
Copyright © 2001 by Lloyd S. Lewan

Cover Design by	Jonde Northcutt
Senior Editor	Kathy Passerine
Editor	Sharyn Markus
Photograph (back cover) by	Robert Weinberg
	Weinberg Photographics
	Denver, Colorado
Printed by	Johnson Printing
	Boulder, Colorado
Published by	Remington Press
	P.O.Box 24187
	Denver, Colorado 80222

ISBN:0-9620360-1-3

FOREWORD

Paul R. Lewan

I want to offer a few opening words about this book because leadership is very important in every business and in every home in America.

The question most often asked of me as a business owner was, "To what do you attribute your success?" I knew in the beginning, and it is still as true today, that the people you serve, those who do the daily work of your company, are the single most important ingredient for success.

Over my career, I have given much time and consideration to finding, keeping, and caring for quality individuals as associates. They are family to me, and that relationship has been essential to the success of the company I was honored to start and to lead these nearly thirty years.

Many factors affect leadership: common sense, strong communication skills, good decision-making, the ability to sell products you believe in, and how well you understand and handle money. But, there is more. I have my faith in God and the love and the support of my wonderful wife and three great children. Without these I would not have been as successful.

I have learned much about leadership from experience; and I have learned much from my brother, Lloyd. He has a keen sense about people and really understands the concept of leadership. He has demonstrated this in every endeavor in which he has been involved. I am proud of him, and I believe what he has written will be a popular desk reference for those who aspire to leadership and for those who are presently in a position of leadership.

Paul Blevins

ACKNOWLEDGMENTS

One who deserves the most credit is my assistant, *Kathy Passerine,* who has been with me each step of the way and without whom I could not have completed this work. I am very grateful to her.

సౌఖ్య

A *special* thank you to those who took the time to comment on my leadership for this book.

సౌఖ్య

My special thanks

to *Jonde Northcutt* for her superb cover design and encouragement,

to *Ron Billingsley* for his invaluable advice and friendship,

and to *Sharyn Markus* for her kindness and excellent editing.

Acknowledgments

For reasons they will understand,
my thanks to

Cinthia Andrews
Fred & Kathy Cannataro
Randy Gradishar
Reverend Leon Kelly
Paul and Marjorie Lewan
Joan Policastri
Robin Powers
Yukimi Sashida
William and Nedra Segall
Stephen Thompson
C. H. Tung and C. C. Tung
John Tymitz
and The Institute for Shipboard Education Staff

DEDICATION

♦ to the thousands of students on Semester at Sea who demanded that I lead them, not just manage them

♦ to my many colleagues at Lewan & Associates, Inc.

♦ to my wonderful nieces and nephew

Kimberly Ann Lewan
Matthew Remington Lewan
Jennifer Elizabeth Lewan

♦ to four of my mentors, none of whom are here today

Edwin Alderson
Ivan Chapman
Merwin Griffiths
Wilfred Landrus

♦ and to those in the world who go without leadership

CONTENTS

Leadership is one of the
most observed and
least understood
phenomena on earth.

James MacGregor Burns

Chapter One

A CALL TO LEADERSHIP

A Call to Leadership

One of the most universal cravings of our time is a hunger for compelling leadership....The crisis of leadership today is the mediocrity or irresponsibility of so many men and women in power....We know far too little about leadership. We fail to grasp the essence of leadership that is relevant to the modern age; and hence, we cannot agree even on the standards by which to measure, recruit, and reject it....Leadership is one of the most observed and least understood phenomena on earth.

This is as true today as it was in 1978 when James MacGregor Burns, who wrote so well on the subject of leadership, penned those words.

Leadership is *the* most important endeavor to which we can aspire. Its significance goes beyond education, career, and training; and it is as important to an organization's success as any other single factor.

Today, the lack of a usable or agreed-upon definition of leadership is as much a factor for the lack of good leadership as is the absence of talent. It is a separate understanding, quite different from management; and without this understanding it is difficult to persuade, to encourage, and to ensure leadership.

I seldom tell this story, but confession is good for the soul. As a young administrator on board ship with an international education program, then known as World Campus Afloat under the auspices of Chapman College, I was confronted with my lack of leadership. A student wrote graffiti about me on one of the public bathroom doors: "Lewan, an overgrown boy scout with a power complex." Unfortunately, he was not too far off. I was acting like a boss, yet trying to be nice to everyone. The comment hurt me deeply, and I worked really hard to give up any role geared toward being liked or toward gaining power. It forced me to be myself, and it helped me to see that there was a difference between leading a voyage and managing a voyage.

As a result, much of my early understanding of leadership came through my involvement with this program, now known as Semester at Sea. Academically affiliated with the University of Pittsburgh for the past twenty years, this program takes university and college students around the world on an ocean liner to introduce them to the peoples and the cultures of our world. Serving in a leadership role for many of these voyages, I was able to see that students wanted to be led, not merely to be managed.

Understanding this difference certainly helped me when I later assumed responsibility in a major office-technology company. I needed to gain a better grasp of leadership; and this took followers, experiences, and the willingness to be humbled. For me this shaping for leadership came through the thousands of students and hundreds of employees I have been privileged to lead.

Perhaps this difference between leadership and management does not make sense to you now, but I hope in reading this book the difference will be clear.

Ultimately, I have learned that leadership is about principles. Anyone who commits to these principles can become a leader at some level. Natural abilities, such as charisma and a commanding voice, make it easier to reach a large group; but leadership is possible without either. What is essential is a commitment to the principles of leadership. Hence, even a quiet, yet wonderful, oboe teacher can be a leader.

A Word to the Reader

This book offers what I have learned and what has served me well over the years. Following are a few observations to keep in mind as you read:

ᘓ Because leadership is important in all endeavors, examples in this book are varied and wide ranging.

ᘓ Most authors on leadership are communicating the same thoughts in different ways, and that is understandable because leadership is the same everywhere. This book is only one more way to think about leadership and one more voice added to the growing body of work about the importance of leadership. A few selected works, for those who choose to read more, are included in the bibliography.

ᔆ Of utmost importance, this book is written to make a strong statement that leadership and management are different skill sets. The science and the value of management are not being lessened by my comments about leadership. Management is as important as leadership for any organization's success, *but* leadership and management are not synonymous.

ᔆ Finally, because leadership is more likely to be practiced when it is understood, this book has been designed to give a broad framework and to provide a practical guide. If you want to follow my thinking carefully, read everything. If you prefer only my thoughts on the practical, skip Chapters Two, Three, and Four and go directly to Chapter Five.

In our country of free and independent citizens, we assume that people like to do their own thing. Yet, most people want someone to show them the way, to set an example for them, or to be their guide. Because we see few examples of great leadership in our daily lives, we often don't know what we are missing. Children, patients, clients, workers, and others simply deserve leadership.

Today, more than ever before, we need leadership in our homes, on our streets, in our organizations, in our neighborhoods, in our businesses, and in our cities. Given the events of September 11, 2001, we can see even more clearly the need for leadership in our nation and around the world. Coping with these events in an appropriate manner will take leadership beyond management worldwide.

∾∿

Losing armies change generals, and they begin to win. Losing football teams change coaches, and they begin to win. Struggling corporations change CEOs, and the corporation begins to improve. *This is the leadership factor.*

PART I

BACKGROUND

Chapter Two

LEADERSHIP IN
CONTEXT

Leadership in Context

Archbishop Desmund Tutu, recipient of the Nobel Peace Prize in 1994 and retired archbishop of Capetown, South Africa, is a man I have been privileged to meet and to dine with several times. He helped me understand the importance of context. At Regis University several years ago, when he was talking about the humiliation suffered by so many in South Africa, he said, "The world suffers so easily from amnesia." These few words stayed with me as a *great context* for his extraordinary struggle and the struggle of his lifetime friend, Nelson Mandela.

As leaders we must have a *context* for our struggle, and finding a context for leadership can best be discovered by understanding today's workplace and by seeing the realities of life faced by today's youth. Understanding what today's workers face and experience will help us appreciate the importance of and the need for good leadership. At the same time, it is imperative that we see the realities of life that our youth face because they represent our *future* leadership.

Today's Workplace

Re-evaluating is important to leadership and to success. Each time I return from a Semester at Sea voyage, I re-examine that which affects the workplace. These are my current findings:

⫻ World economies are coming together, but world peoples are not.

⫻ Loyalty between corporations and their workers, both ways, is decreasing.

⫻ Many workers seem overwhelmed with the complexity of their lives.

⫻ More workers are overworked, yet under-utilized.

- The workforce is older; and the young will have to adjust and, in a sense, be burdened by this fact.

- The workplace is more culturally diverse and portrays the world as it really is.

- Fewer workers come to work emotionally healthy and happy because of stress in their lives outside of work. With limited benefit dollars, the workplace struggles with how to help.

- In settling disagreements and disputes, litigious procedures have replaced good-will, good faith, and good manners. Therefore, forgiveness and apology are less attractive strategies.

- Talent paths are replacing career paths.

Several gurus in leadership and organizational management offer these comments about the workplace:

- Peter F. Druker in *Post-Capitalist Society* indicates: "Already an estimated two-thirds of U. S. employees work in the service sector, and 'knowledge' is becoming a most important product. This calls for different organizations as well as different leaders of workers."

⫻ Warren Bennis, the noted author, suggests the following about the high-tech future: "The factory of the future will have only two employees, a man and a dog. The man will feed the dog, and the dog will keep the man from touching the equipment."

In my dealings with human-resources issues, I came across a great little employee handbook put out by Pritchett and Associates of Dallas, Texas. While many trends were identified, four are summarized below:

⫻ In the coming era, jobs will be tasks you do, not something you have.

⫻ Conventional full-time insiders will be the new minority in the workplace. Self-employed consultants, independent contractors, job shares, part-timers, and outsourcers will be the future majority.

⫽ In the last twenty years, nearly half of our companies were restructured; nearly one hundred were acquired or merged; many more were downsized; and over one million sought bankruptcy or failed.

⫽ Modern technology will contribute considerably to job imbalance.

Involved with an inner-city program aimed at preventing at-risk young people from joining gangs, I see the gap between the have's and the have not's (a gap that is so common to the third world) growing ever wider in America. We must work hard to ensure that these groups do not become too disparate economically and socially, and this reconciliation will take leadership.

Many workers today are doing as they are told; few follow anyone. As a new second lieutenant in the Marine Corps, I was saluted by some men with silent contempt: "Yes, Sir, Lieutenant," emphasis on "lieutenant." It took a little experience and learning on my part before their salute changed to, "Aye, aye, Skipper," with warmth. This was my first introduction to the difference between managing and leading.

One additional observation about today's workplace can be seen in the different priorities that exist in each generation.

※ In a talk Henry Kissinger gave at the University of Denver, he suggested that today's generation is different. They are more motivated by social issues, the environment, unemployment, and racial equality than the previous generations who were trying to make it economically.

※ "Values age and narrow," notes author and speaker Tom Peters.

※ In the magazine *Training*, July 2000, Ron Zemke wrote: "Welcome to the new generation gap – the broadest range of age and value of employees in American history – and they are being asked to work together cubicle to cubicle and get along in the bargain."

The workplace *is* changing; and with these changes will come confusion, disconnection, and frustration on the part of many workers. Today's employees will adjust better and be more productive if *led* through these changing workplace characteristics.

Today's Youth

Let me also offer a context for our youth because they will govern, will determine, and will decide the quality of our later years and the quality of life of those who follow us. Although we are challenged daily by the growing number of at-risk youth, *most of today's young people deserve our respect and faith;* and I, for one, have great faith in their ability to lead the future. This faith is absolute and is based upon my years with university and college men and women.

Young people today, in America in particular, are blessed with affluence, opportunities, and freedoms that are extraordinary. Yet, these same young people will be asked during their lifetimes to make more choices about more issues than any previous generation. Consider the following:

ℓ They will be asked to make choices about national leadership in a time when the price of committed, dedicated national leadership is very high in terms of family, health, and personal finance.

⫽ They will be asked to make choices about family life – whether to marry, to have children, and, if so, at what age and at what expense to their professional lives – in a period where fewer traditional, family-role models are available to them.

⫽ They live in a time of confusing priorities when athletes and broadcasters make more money than scientists, artists, and teachers and when global military expenditures exceed the income of the poorer half of humanity.

⫽ They live in a world where tension exists between technology and science and public policy and in a time when they wonder if we have the human skills to manage the technology that we have created.

⫽ They live in an instant generation: instant food, instant abortion, instant communication, instant divorce, and instant foreign policy. They watch leaders who often have to make quick decisions with biased and erroneous data.

⫽ They live in a time when there are a growing variety of acceptable behaviors in society against which to test their young belief systems.

⫽ They live in a time when the press and the other media often dwell on the sensational and the negative.

⫽ They face a knowledge explosion in the information and service age that is almost unthinkable. At the same time, they have been asked to have a conscience for others — a conscience about the aging, the dying, unwed mothers, street children, Vietnam and Gulf War veterans, suicidal teenagers, the unborn, women and other minorities, criminals, victims of crime, the homeless, animals, homosexuals, substance abusers, single parents and their children, abused children and women, rape victims, AIDS victims, and the list goes on.

If we think this is anything approaching the full list of challenges facing our young, we are not watching, reading, or listening. This is only one half.

The other half, represented by other nations, are the challenges of our *interdependent world.*

⫽ The young today have become aware of this encroaching international arena as America's competitive edge is being challenged on a number of fronts. Even though America should remain the world's major super power for some years, China, and perhaps others, will gain similar status. Do you speak Mandarin?

⫽ Today's youth hope for a stable economy during their lives. Yet, they know that the disenfranchised people on the earth grow in numbers daily and realize that if these people cannot meet their basic needs they will have no choice but to rebel.

Recently, I read a perspective by The League of Women Voters describing the international future our young people face. It stated:

> If we could shrink the population on earth to a village of precisely one-hundred people, with human ratios remaining the same, seventy [people] would be unable to read,

fifty would be suffering from malnutrition, eighty would live in substandard housing, and only one would have a university education.

Our young will face a highly interdependent world of eight billion people. Is it any wonder that they are searching for their own identity with fads, body piercing, and tattoos?

The kicker is that our young are neither prepared nor adequately educated for this complex reality of interdependence. Dr. Harold Taylor, a friend and a man much wiser than I, wrote: "Either we educate them for this reality of interdependence, or we miseducate them. There is no neutrality."

Having said all of this, *am I discouraged? Absolutely not.* These challenges will force youth to focus on the art of leadership. As with all youth before them, they are lovably idealistic, wonderfully naïve, and impertinently impatient. They have the talent, thank goodness; and they will face the future and will ensure that civilization and reason will prevail. Have no doubt about this!

We must step up to help the young accomplish these challenges *by providing and encouraging leadership.* We must also *earn* their loyalty; it is not guaranteed.

A Final Thought about Context

In *As Time Goes On,* an unknown author spelled out a paradox of our time in history. In part, s/he wrote,

> We have taller buildings but shorter tempers,
> Wider freeways but narrower viewpoints.
> We buy more but enjoy it less.
> We have bigger houses and smaller families.
> We have more degrees but less sense.
> We've learned to make a living but not a life.
> We have been to the moon and back,
> But have trouble meeting a new neighbor.
> We've split the atom but not our prejudices.
> These are times of tall men and short character,
> Very steep profits and shallow relationships,
> Of fancier homes but more broken homes...

Author and speaker, Stephen R. Covey suggests, generally, that there are only three constants: change, principles, and the power to adapt to these two. Yes, this *is* what leadership is about and why Stephen Covey has been so well read. He is on target!

Change is inevitable. When it occurs, a leader can really make a difference. Therefore, leaders must watch change, which is really context. They must inspect what they expect. In short, *leadership is not a spectator sport.*

As we look at a context for leadership today, I finish this chapter with this thought: Most of life is cyclical, for example, the economy, real-estate, relationships, biorhythms, and politics. Leaders instinctively look for the cycle, the rhythm, and prepare for it. This is a part of understanding context.

Chapter Three

LEADERSHIP vs.
MANAGEMENT

Leadership vs. Management

An important reason for this book is to distinguish leadership from management – that is, how an organization is governed. My emphasis will be on the leadership half.

Let me state the obvious before I continue: A business must be profitable and successful long term. Leadership and management are key to this objective, but each is key in a separate way.

Leadership is Qualitative.
Management is Quantitative.

In the simplest of terms, leadership is responsible for the relationships of a business or organization; and management is responsible for the daily operations and the efficiency of a business or organization. Both are important, and both are needed; but confusion often exists between the two.

Management

First, let's take a quick look at management. Management is loosely described by most, beginning with early classical management theorists up to today's Peter Druker, as the function of planning, organizing, staffing, directing, and controlling. It is a specific skill for a specific work – accounting, information technology, or marketing, among others. In his latest book, *Management Challenges for the 21st Century*, Druker even more clearly states, "Management exists for the sake of the institution's results."

Dr. David R. Anderson, Dennis J. Sweeney, and Thomas A. Williams, in their book *An Introduction to Management Science*, probably typify today's definition of management with their opening statement:

Management science, an approach to managerial decision-making that is based on scientific method, makes extensive use of quantitative analysis....Today many use the terms operations research and management science interchangeably.

Leadership

Whereas management is the science of business, leadership is the art of business.

Both are important!
Both are needed!
But, there is a difference!

An organization/business will never achieve results without a commitment to the people within the organization/business. Hence, leadership must go beyond management.

I am a big fan of the Daniels School of Business at the University of Denver. A few years back, the business school decided to revamp their graduate business curriculum. Today, they have an exciting set of programs and degrees. Much was based on the following quote, a small part of a steering document:

For more than a decade, criticisms of management education have been remarkably consistent: MBA programs graduate persons who excel technically, but who are managerially handicapped. That is, they seem to lack those skills critical to individual and organizational success. They are fine technicians but poor leaders; they can solve problems, but they cannot communicate their solutions; and they lack a global perspective, a meaningful value structure, creativity, and a sense of genuine humanity.

This statement is highly qualitative and only encouraged me to continue the separation between leadership and management that I am attempting to make and to awaken in this book.

For years our bookstores had "management" signs over a section in their stores, but only in the past decade has leadership appeared with a sign of its own. In fact, leadership is now an industry – books, tapes, and speeches. I am not interested in the industry of leadership, just the importance of and the need for a definition of leadership in relation to management.

In America we often substitute management for leadership without notice. *I want you to take notice. There is a difference.*

You must understand *both* leadership and management to ensure that both are present in an organization, a government, a home, or elsewhere. *Leadership is not management and vice versa. Leaders make sure management is in place; it is not generally the other way around.*

What I have learned most about the distinction between leadership and management is that leadership is a universal skill, the same everywhere, and that management is a cultural skill, different in different organizations. For example, IBM has one culture; and their planning, organizing, and regulating may be quite different from the planning, organizing, and regulating of Hewlett-Packard or that of the Roman Catholic Church. This is understandable because management has to fit the organization's culture.

Do not assume that both come from the same person, either. At times, yes, but it is not as likely as our tables of organization and literature suggest. Leadership is not embodied in a style, a technique, or a label. Rather, it is embodied in a person. This helps explain why an electronics firm goes to a cookie company to find a CEO (leader). They want leadership and will look anywhere.

Secretary of State, retired General Colin L. Powell, in *18 Lessons from a Very Successful Leader,* says much about leadership. His comments are particularly important in revealing definite distinctions between leadership and management:

> Leadership is the art of accomplishing more than the science of management says is possible.

> Organization charts and fancy titles count for next to nothing.

> Theories of management don't much matter. Endeavors succeed or fail because of the people involved. Only by attracting the best people will you accomplish great deeds.

One of the dangers I see is that leadership is often described as a managerial role. For example, Henry Mintzberg, a professor of organizational management, suggested some of these types: figurehead, motivator, liaison, disseminator, monitor, spokesperson, disturbance handler, resource allocator, and negotiator, among others.

Our Judeo-Christian heritage talks of leadership: "How much better to get wisdom than gold" (Proverbs 16:16). Wisdom, not efficiency, is at the heart of leadership.

Jack Welch, the well-known CEO of General Electric until recently, says in part:

> Good business leaders create a vision, articulate the vision, passionately own the vision, and relentlessly drive it to completion. Above all else, though, good leaders are open, and they are straight with people.

In their hallmark work *Learning to Lead,* Warren Bennis and Joan Goldsmith suggest four character traits (at least three of which are qualitative) that people demand from their leaders:

1. Purpose, direction, and meaning
2. Trust
3. Optimism
4. Action and results

Abraham Zaleznik states in his book, *The Managerial Mystic: Restoring Leadership in Business*:

> True leaders are rare in business….many executives, who were once potential leaders, have instead become absorbed by the managerial mystique. The mystique requires dedication to process, structures, roles, and indirect forms of communication. It discourages ideas, people, convictions, and direct talk.

In an article entitled *Leadership Defined*, Isabel Lopez, a Denver resident, writes: "We discuss leadership today because of the lack of leaders and not because of the abundance."

Stephen Covey says, "Management works *in* the system. Leadership works *on* the system" (italics added).

A distinguished scholar in Denver, Marshall Kaplan argues: "Leaders are willing not only to stand up and be counted, but to ask us to be counted along with them. Because of them most of us become better than who and what we are."

Leadership is lofty, yes, but essential.

So much has seduced us away from what leadership truly is. In an article entitled "A Ticket to Ride," Kristine Ellis notes: "From total quality management and the balance scoreboard to emotional intelligence, corporations continue to buy seats on the 'magic bullet,' the roller coaster of organizational development trends."

United Technologies Corporation of Hartford, Connecticut, published a message in the *Wall Street Journal* entitled "Let's Get Rid of Management."

No end exists to the books and the articles written about and the speeches and the ideas spoken about leadership and management to *suggest* that they are different. The distinction, however, is clearer and easier in writing than in actual practice.

Leadership in our literature and educational institutions changes depending on time and circumstances. (This reminds me of the training for shark attacks. In the early days we were told to make a lot of noise, to kick, and to hit. Now, we are told not to move, to be still in the water.) In the beginning leadership was taught by listing the traits of a leader. Personal behaviors were enough. With the growing human-resources movement in the '60's and beyond and the strong emphasis on management styles, buzz words became very popular, for example, "empowering," "participative," "corporate culture," "re-engineering." I haven't enough space to include them all. Today, the growing movement is to discuss leadership in terms of the situation, a relative look. The leader decides what to do, depending on who is involved or what is going on in the particular situation.

This is all good because some real strength lies in these logics, but it is not enough.

Therefore, let me add my little piece, certainly no better than others and only my contribution to all that is out there. It is the *juxtaposition* of leadership and management that I am interested in.

Three notions – vision, focus, and influence – constitute and summarize leadership and expressly separate it from management.

Vision

Turn me on and get me excited about something I can grasp.

Focus

Put what is really important in the spotlight for me and make sure we accomplish the mission.

Influence

Show me your motive to gain influence and engagement with me and to earn my trust.

And, all three notions presuppose character. Personal character has no substitute because in the end it is a *person*, the leader, who makes a well-defined organization come alive. Consider the following three comments about the importance of a person:

✎ "Nothing is so strong as gentleness, and nothing is so gentle as real strength," noted Francis DeSales, a 17th Century French bishop. I believe he understood leadership. Don't you?

/// Units *and* people receive medals in the military, but it is always the leader who reconciles people to a unit's mission.

/// Businessman and philanthropist, John D. Rockefeller, Sr. once said, "I will pay more for the ability to deal with people than any other ability under the sun."

Perhaps the best-known example in early organizational studies of the importance of what motivates a worker was with the Western Electric Company of Hawthorne, Illinois. Developed by Elton Mayo, these studies came to be known as the Hawthorne studies. In short, employees were given extras (for example, lighting) to motivate them. Productivity did improve; but, when the extras were taken away, productivity continued to increase. The extra attention and the human interaction proved to be the motivators, not the extras.

In the final analysis, leadership is a *presence* in one's life. It is not about presents (always giving something, for example benefits). It is about being in a person's life – personally or in a group sense.

I close this chapter with a number of examples, for it is this issue of *presence* that is key to the distinction between leadership and management. Please note that I did not say *perfection, just presence.*

◆ I started my undergraduate work at the University of Denver not knowing what major to pursue. General business made sense. In my first week on campus, I met with the head of the accounting department, a legend then, the late Wayne Shroyer. He was nice to me, offered me a job as his grader, and "told me" that I was an accounting major. Liking him immediately and in the absence of a solid idea about a major, I followed his input. He was a great leader, and having him for a mentor served me well. His presence was enough.

◆ Last fall I received this kind note from a student on Semester at Sea: "You didn't know me, but you affected my life tremendously. I trusted you and felt like my dad was with me...." Presence.

◆   I watched a divorced father in McDonalds the other evening when I stopped for a cup of coffee. He bought his daughter extra upon extra each time she asked for something – a milkshake, more fries. He asked her at least five times if there was anything else she wanted. One could see by her actions and eyes that she wanted him to look, to touch, and to be with her. She wanted his presence, not just his presents. (Isn't this the lament of so many children in broken homes? They want their parents to be in their lives, not just to buy them presents.)

◆   In the mid '80's, our ship went aground while coming into the port of Alexandria, Egypt. We faced a difficult moment. The United States Ambassador and high-level Egyptian navy and government officials were involved and assisting as we took on water. Standing on the bridge, the captain and the chief engineer, both Chinese, were deciding whether to shut down the boilers. We were a steam turbine ship, and it was imperative that the seawater not reach the boilers. Since we would relinquish power by shutting down the boilers, this was a difficult decision.

Some of our students, faculty, and staff were frightened; and, of course, for precautionary reasons we had everyone put on life jackets.

I could not help thinking to myself, "What good would the *One Minute Manager* do us now – one minute goal setting, one minute praising, one minute reprimand, and more." I appreciate Ken Blanchard's work, and this is not a reflection on this work or his great thinking. But, we needed leadership (presence) beyond management at that point in time, and we got it.

◆ The Institute for Shipboard Education is extremely careful in the selection of the person appointed as executive dean on a Semester at Sea voyage because of the responsibility and the potentially difficult times: the daily nagging, the pressure of nearly one thousand people living on a ship, sea sickness, the support of dozens of academic courses, limited space and the lack of personal space, incredibly hard work, the primary focus always on the programs and the possibilities in the ports of call, an international crew, and the fact that most of the people on board ship have not met each other prior to sailing. This requires more than management skill. It requires the right person (leader) to bring and to hold it all together.

◆　Pilots on a 747 airliner have many management functions to perform while in the air that are extremely important to the safety and the operation of the flight. Yet, if something goes wrong during the flight, most want a leader, experienced and wise, in the pilot's seat.

◆　Not too long ago, I was sitting in church a few weeks after the founding pastor moved on. It is a special church with a mission to help reconcile urban and suburban churches. The former pastor is a friend. There is a big hole in the church and in the hearts of all who attend. Is this bad? No. Is it permanent? No. Is it lethal? No. Another pastor will be called, but it does reinforce for me the value and the importance of *leadership* in the *presence of a person.*

The world is changing rapidly, and it will take leadership beyond management to keep our lives and our economy healthy. In the end leadership is about *principles applied consistently by quality people, with appropriate motives, who care and who have a mission in mind.*

Chapter Four

ENTREPRENEUR vs.
BUREAUCRAT

Entrepreneur vs. Bureaucrat

Lately, many corporations have suffered tough times. While the reasons have varied, some of this downturn can be attributed to a failure of leadership in these corporations, a failure of leadership hampered by bureaucratic in-fighting.

A major battle in the workplace in the early 21st Century will be the battle between the entrepreneurial and the bureaucratic spirits of doing business – that is, how an organization organizes itself to conduct activities. For example, in highly bureaucratic organizations greater interest is focused on management, which often lessens the focus on leadership.

Although natural tension exists between the entrepreneurial and the bureaucratic spirits, both are needed in all organizations; and they are represented in leadership (subjective man) and management (objective man). Let me defend this notion.

Sometimes the organizational form overshadows the ideology (the belief) behind an organization. This is bureaucracy. Drawing from Max Weber and Jacob W. Getzels, the noted sociologists, among other organizational theorists, let me oversimplify complex formal organizational theory. Although this is dangerous, it is necessary in order to understand the nature of leadership.

The early outline of bureaucracy as an organizational form included many characteristics and many warnings. The central core ideas formed around the following notions:

- **Hierarchy of Authority**
  Chain of command is essential.

- **Functional Specificity**
  You have a specific job. Stay inside that description.

- **Rules and Regulations**
  Everything is communicated in written regulations. This is how you control.

- **Universalistic**
  Nothing is personal. It is just business – lacking affection or enthusiasm.

- **Rational Authority**
  Rank and power are given and strictly enforced by the organization and are always titled – for example, colonel or vice president.

Theorists also acknowledged the other ends of these dimensions:

- Roles that are functionally specific may be replaced by functional diffusion (multitasked).

- Authority that is rational may be replaced by charismatic authority.

- Affectivity that is impersonal may become particularistic or personal.

While this is a thumbnail and sketchy look at bureaucracy, it also suggests that other organizational forms or spirits exist. For example, entrepreneurship is the other end of the governance continuum.

Webster's New Universal Unabridged Dictionary defines the bureaucrat as "an official who works by fixed routine without exercising intelligent judgment." An entrepreneur, defines Webster in the same dictionary, is "a person who organizes and manages an enterprise, esp. a business, usually with considerable initiative and risk." Clearly the definitions are different; and, more importantly, they each imply a different spirit.

My bottom line is this: Bureaucrats often acknowledge many of the same concepts as entrepreneurs – customer service, people count, and accomplishment of goals. Definitions are close; but behind these two ways of doing business is a different *attitude*, an attitude that shows only by looking at the ones being *served*.

For example, those who are efficient tend to have more bureaucratic spirits; but, in reality, they can also have very entrepreneurial spirits. A look at their motive will tell. If it is the customer and good service first, then all the efficiency in the world is fine. In fact, it is valuable.

Let me attempt to make this spirit of service understandable with several examples.

- ☐ In a local health-food restaurant that I visited recently, no receptionist was present. Because the sign told me to wait, I waited and waited. Sitting at the "group table" was a waitperson who was obviously chatting with a friend who had come in to see her. She looked me right in the eye, at least four times, but made no attempt to find anyone or to call out to me that someone would be with me in a minute. Entrepreneurial or bureaucratic spirit? You decide.

- ☐ Some time ago, I called a large cable company, a company with no competition. After letting the phone ring forty-three times (yes, I really did count), I grew disgusted and hung up. I was calling to debate my bill. My cable service was disconnected the next Saturday. When I finally reached a service representative the following Monday, he said that I needed to come in to resolve the issue. Of course, the cable would remain off until I came in. Tell me. Is this good business? This method and this attitude told me the motive. It sure wasn't customer service.

☐ In our place of business, we attempt to answer phones within a few rings and to transfer the caller to the appropriate person immediately – and all with a great attitude. Even if customers are way off base with their concerns or comments, they are customers. We are entrepreneurs, and we always serve.

The motive toward those you serve shows in your attitude, and the battle I am suggesting is between the entrepreneurial attitude and the bureaucratic attitude. I am sure you know what I mean and have many examples of your own.

Entrepreneurship and bureaucracy are not always about large versus small. Although there is a greater likelihood of finding more bureaucracy in very large organizations, entrepreneurial spirits do thrive in large organizations. Quality companies who are successful have kept their entrepreneurial spirit – service, service, service.

Unfortunately, while many large organizations try to keep a good "entrepreneurial" attitude, many have lousy attitudes toward those whom they serve. Often, they are more interested in maximizing their own profit, power, and position than in serving their customers – that is until business starts to fall off.

Because my driver's license had expired, I went to the division of motor vehicle to renew it. Waiting patiently for an hour, I stood in the line that said "license renewal." When I reached the person at the counter, he was chatting with his colleague in the next booth (even though the line was very long). When he finally turned to me, he said, "You are in the wrong line. You need to go to line six – new licenses."

Now, did I do something wrong? Did I read the sign wrong? Am I not an important client? Again, there is a spirit of doing business; and it shows in the way clients are served. How about, "I'm so sorry our signs are not more explanatory, Mr. Lewan. Here is the correct form. They can help you in line six; but, if I finish here, I'll try to help." Saying anything to let me know that I counted, even if I was confused as to which line to stand in, would have sent a customer-oriented message.

A salesperson and I arrived at a large mortgage company to see if we could offer our counsel or our services for their office-technology needs. The receptionist treated us like we were the "plague." She obviously disliked salespeople and thought we were the lowest. She did not know that I was personally acquainted with her CEO, which is why I was along. I did not offer that information, for that would have been arrogant on my part.

Regardless, what attitude was this young woman showing? We did not feel welcomed or valued. Would it not have been better to have replied, "Would you be willing to wait until I have a moment? Then I will see if someone has time to see you." How did she know we were not a customer of theirs? You get the point.

Two spirits, entrepreneurial and bureaucratic, have, in my judgment, two different priorities toward customers. This may seem like a stretch, but think about it. It is an important part of the philosophy of business.

An early industrial organizational theorist, Douglas McGregor offered "Theory X – Theory Y" as underlying assumptions for motivating employees. Theory X holds that most people prefer to be directed and are not interested in responsibility. They want safety and security. Managers who hold to Theory X tend to control and to structure workplaces. They tend to assume employees are unreliable, immature, and irresponsible. Advocates of Theory Y assume the opposite and will encourage employees to be more creative and productive. If treated right, employees are capable of more. This style assumes that work is as natural as play and that people have to feel esteem to be productive.

Obviously, I believe that leaders must be Theory Y persons and that entrepreneurial organizations are generally Theory Y advocates.

When I began my doctoral studies in higher education at Oklahoma State University, I was fascinated by the study of complex organizations. One of my mentors suggested I visit the library to read all I could about organizations, leadership, and management to help frame my thinking. The first book I picked up (and this dates me terribly) was *The Bureaucratic Experience* by Ralph Hummel. The impact of his book has stayed with me all these years.

Hummel suggests that human beings have moved from human systems to organizational systems. He says this is understandable, for what is important to organizational systems known as bureaucracies is not always the same as what is important to society. As an example, Hummel argues that calculability of results (efficiency) is important to bureaucracy but that happiness and gratification are important to society. Although this is a little "heady" to think about, it is so very important to leadership. *Reconciling organizational results with the gratification of the followers is at the heart of leadership.*

In the book's final chapter, "Bureaucracy: the Terminal World," Hummel offers:

> You can recognize bureaucracy invading your organization when cases replace people, functions replace actions and social relations, means replace ends, operational code replaces social norms, roles replace persons,

commands replace dialogue, functionaries replace citizens, and most importantly, *management replaces leadership* (italics added).

While I could quote other authors who have addressed pieces of this, I will not. By now you have the point: *An attitude is implied in how you organize and in how you govern.*

In an article entitled "Haley's Leadership U-Turn," published in the *Harvard Business Review,* July–August, 2000, Rich Teerlink, President and COO of the Harley Davidson Motorcycle division in 1987, wrote: "Even if you are hardwired to be a leader who shares power rather than exert it, the command and control model is hard to avoid."

Bureaucracy is a power instrument of the first order for the one who is in control, and it can easily reduce human effectiveness. Aldous Huxley in *Brave New World* knew a world in which not the brave but the dehumanized would survive – bureaucracy.

Let me suggest from my daily life how the entrepreneurial spirit is different from the bureaucratic spirit.

☐ In our business we decide what makes sense and seems appropriate. Then we call our attorney and ask, "Are we all right?" The bureaucrat calls the firm attorney first and asks, "What should we do?"

☐ A small group of salespeople take my office to host a luncheon with a customer. But, first they ask me to stay a few minutes to say "hi." I also stay to serve the soft drinks to whoever has been invited – administrator, purchasing agent, or CEO. This is the entrepreneurial spirit. Service, first.

☐ On passing our communication center one day, where all our incoming calls are received and handled or passed on for action, I heard one young woman say, "There is no supervisor here right now."

She meant well; and when she got off the phone, I commented, "You are authorized to say, 'I am the duty person today. Let me try to help you.' "

She said, "Is that okay?"

I responded, "You bet. The customer is our focus, and you may 'own' the call." This is the entrepreneurial spirit.

☐ When I am "preaching" to one of our very best copier salespersons, Ann Brecke, she will sign a "T" with her hands indicating time out. This is not because she is not interested in what I am saying. (I hope.) Rather, she has an appointment with a customer and has to leave. She always has appointments with customers, and we both know she has the right priorities. We have the entrepreneurial spirit.

In his book *Innovation and Entrepreneurship,* Peter F. Druker said, "The new technology is entrepreneurial management." Is this an attempt to combine these spirits?

What is the point of all this? The entrepreneurial spirit thrives on leadership; the bureaucratic spirit thrives on management. The danger in the bureaucratic spirit is that we are likely to continue our one-directional system of decrees, rather than a trusted relationship between leader and follower.

Favoring an entrepreneurial spirit, I share an idea from an article, "The Glass Ceiling – Another View," that I wrote a few years ago for a newspaper. Quite accurately, women argue that they are often held back by a "glass ceiling." My point in the article was that the entrepreneur has also been held back. Women make great entrepreneurs. They don't give up easily, they work hard, they do not care about title or status, they are self-motivated, and they prefer to tackle a task their own way. A look at national and at state statistics, particularly statistics in Colorado, reveal that women start enterprises at a rate equal to men and that they seem to stay in business longer than men. *Hence, women and entrepreneurs (men and women) often suffer the same fate in the hands of bureaucrats.*

I want to be led, not merely to be managed; and I'll say it one more time: Management is good, but there is more – leadership. In fact, leadership will become increasingly sought after in the next decade as a skill separate from management. Really successful organizations in the 21st Century will have to know the difference. In the end the entrepreneurial spirit demands leadership first. The bureaucratic spirit prefers management.

A large percentage of all new jobs in America are with companies that have fewer than several hundred employees. As new university graduates and others changing jobs look for employment, they are much more likely to find the need for an entrepreneurial spirit than for a bureaucratic spirit. Therefore, they need to know where they are in this debate of "spirits" before selecting a place to work. It will make a huge difference to their success and satisfaction.

Again, the only really good clue in discerning this difference is watching how those who govern *view* those they should be serving, inside and outside the organization – employees and customers!

To dot the "i" on this chapter, admitting that it falls so short of a serious discussion of complex organizations, here are a few final points:

Years ago, Mr. James G. Anderson, then with Johns Hopkins University, wrote a piece for the *Educational Administration Quarterly*. The promise of his research was what interested me most, and I quote:

> In this paper the functioning of bureaucratic rules is examined within complex organizations with particular application to the school. Rules are considered as barriers of organizational authority, controlling and directing actions of participants in the accomplishment of a common goal through specification, communication, impersonalization, and differential implementation. In attempting, however, to structure and impersonalize relationships so that the individual personalities will have little effect on the accomplishment of organizational goals, the ground work is laid for dysfunction within the organization. Many of these dysfunctional elements may be viewed as a direct outgrowth of the attempt to impersonalize organizational relationships and to delineate authority and responsibility *inherent* in individual offices through a body of rules.

This is so true. All too often rules detract from creativity. In fact, I jotted another definition for bureaucracy from a dictionary (although I cannot recall which one):

bureaucracy: a system of administration marked by constant thriving for increased functions and power, by lack of initiative and flexibility, by indifference to human needs and public opinion, and by a tendency to defer decisions to superiors or to impede action with red tape.

છ-૭

It is in the "spirit" defined in this chapter as either entrepreneurial or bureaucratic that we see a different emphasis on service. Therefore, leaders must decide which spirit best supports their organization. There is a difference.

Chapter Five

ABOUT LEADERSHIP

About Leadership

Thus far I have attempted to offer a framework for a quick look at leadership as distinguished from management. Before I move on to my own definition of leadership, I want to offer some very clear statements about leadership that add to this framework and that further distinguish leadership from management.

Leadership Is a Personal Choice
&ao&

Leadership is a free-will offering. It signifies a commitment you are making. To serve as a leader, you first must raise your hand to indicate you want to be considered for leadership.

In the company I see as ideal (and we have tried hard to do this in our firm), it is important to train all supervisory personnel for an activity that the business is engaged in, such as purchasing, sales, human resources, or accounts receivable. But, then it is important to offer those in the group who ask to be more (a leader) a different track designed specifically to prepare them as leaders beyond management.

In essence, two tracks, leadership and management, exist. This sounds silly, sort of a two-tiered system; but it really is not. To assume that leadership and management are the same is what is silly. Both leadership and management are important, but they are distinctly different.

Leadership is as much a calling, a willingness, and a commitment as it is a skill. When leaving the United States Marine Corps in my mid-twenties, I joined Chapman College in Orange County, California. As mentioned earlier, I had the opportunity to join their unique floating university program, known first as the University of the Seven Seas and later as World Campus Afloat-Chapman College.

When asked by the powers-that-be, "Are you good with kids?" I answered, "Yes," figuring that young marines were kids. When asked, "Do you know anything about ships?" once again I replied, "Yes." Afterall, I had traveled to Southeast Asia on a ship and spent a month or so on a helicopter carrier, the *Princeton*. To the question, "Can you take young college students around the world on a ship?" I thought, "You bet!" reflecting on how unprepared many military men and women were to live in a foreign culture. Seeing this as my chance to lead in an international setting, I raised my hand!

I had just finished my master's degree, but I raised my hand anyway. Joining the team as an administrator and later as a shipboard dean, I have been involved ever since in some capacity.

In *The Leadership Secrets of Attila the Hun*, Wes Roberts suggests that you must have the "lust for leadership." In other words, you have to want to lead. I would not say it that way, but it does reinforce that a choice must be made to lead.

You must also be willing to make the many sacrifices it requires to be a leader, and these sacrifices will become more apparent as you go further into this text.

You never know who might be interested in leadership. Keep your eyes *wide* open. Someone who has talent may be raising his/her hand. Talent can be overlooked, especially leadership talent. It is good that someone took a risk on these three. It has been reported that

☑ after Fred Astaire's first screen test, a 1933 memo from a MGM casting director stated, "Can't act. Slightly bald. Can dance a little;"

☑ an expert once said of Vince Lombardi: "He possesses minimal football knowledge, lacks motivation;"

☑ a newspaper fired Walt Disney because he lacked ideas.

Leadership Is about Principles
ʚ•ɞ

Math has theorems, religions have commandments, physics has laws, science adheres to a scientific method, medicine has strict standards, and *leadership has principles*. A person can only claim the name "leader" when s/he adheres to the principles of leadership. A leader always acts out of principle, not from revenge or from what others consider fair. Leaders do not keep score as to who has done what and how many times.

You cannot be elected or appointed to leadership. You can be elected to an office or appointed to a position, but you must earn the right to be a leader by adhering to principles.

As a young Marine Corps officer, I learned early the principles of leadership. Many principles remain with me to this day; but I offer only two, herein, for they have served me well in every position of leadership that I have been privileged to hold:

☑ *Eat last!*
Those whom you serve eat (come) first. What a simple but great principle. It has been ingrained in me for so long that I even take communion last at my church.

☑ *Familiarity breeds contempt!*
Be friendly, but not familiar. Followers

want to trust and to respect you; and when your conversations and actions become too familiar, you reduce your ability to lead. It is a hard road for a leader to be a part of something and apart from it to guarantee objective, impartial leadership. Selective humanness is okay, but accept the reality that leadership is lonely and necessarily so.

Having wonderful colleagues at our company, I attend events and important functions (marriages, christenings, funerals) in their lives; but I do not *hang around* with them. A good leader is never a good buddy. Rather, a good leader is a trusted colleague. There is a difference. Go home if you need to be loved or are in need of a friend.

As executive dean on the ship, I rarely visit cabins for social times or join the usual chat groups enjoyed by faculty, staff, and students. My role is to be fair, objective, mission-focused, and friendly – not familiar.

You can't step over this line. Although this is hard to live by and many would say it is ridiculous, not human, I say it is worth it. Think about it, please.

People will not follow you, even if you have a charismatic style or great rhetoric, if you do not adhere to the principles of leadership. They will not trust you. A leader acts from principles. Always.

Leaders Know How They Perform
☙~❧

Few individuals have the experience to completely or adequately evaluate a leader's performance. At the end of a voyage, students have an opportunity to rate my performance, as do the faculty and the staff. My colleagues back in the home office also offer advice as to my performance. While these other evaluations help tremendously, in the end, *I know* whether I did a good job.

For example, the students on one voyage gave me high marks. I gave myself an average mark because I did not do two things well enough. I did not earn the rapport with the faculty I should have, and I did not spend enough time with the student-life staff. Had I put forth more effort with both of these important groups, I would have given myself a higher mark.

Leadership Implies Learning, As Well As Leading; Otherwise, a Leader Can Become Quite Arrogant

ॐॐ

On one Semester at Sea voyage, I had a delightful, very competent student-life director from Chicago. She is an African-American woman, and I learned a great deal from her.

While our ship was docked in Kenya, I was standing on the pier talking with the many vendors, many of whom I have known for years, as they set up their shops with a variety of East-African artifacts and souvenirs. As she was coming off the gangway, I offered all I knew about her, proudly, to some of the vendors who inquired about her. After all, she was an African-American woman in an important position visiting an African nation; and they were curious.

She heard me as we were only a few feet from the gangway. She walked over; and with a smile and a hug, she whispered in my ear, "Why didn't you just introduce me and let me define myself?" Good advice, especially for a man!

I learned a very important principle. A leader should be open to all new lessons, however slight.

Leadership Cannot Be Taught

You must see and must experience a good leader to really know what leadership is about because leadership is a skill that is passed on and developed through mentoring. Mentoring is a relationship where one person, because of individual gifts and strengths, helps another person in the same area. Webster defines mentor as a trusted guide, tutor, or coach.

As one reviews the curricular offerings of most college and university schools of business, generally, many more courses in management than in leadership are offered. Why? Management is a science for which it is much easier to develop curriculum and to teach. Management is considered an essential tool of business, as with marketing or information technology. In contrast, the art of business – sales, entrepreneurship, and leadership – is harder to develop curriculum for and to teach.

Generally, only the principles can be taught; and to really learn the art of business, you have to watch someone do it, be mentored, and then gain experience. The best analogy of this is parenting. Parents talk a lot, but children learn about parenting by watching and by experiencing their parents.

Leadership Has Limits
એ⊷ક

As a leader, I do not act upon ninety percent of what I casually hear or see. Rather, I log it away and only act when it is appropriate and important to the mission. This is a tough one.

Moreover, a leader never capitalizes on the weaknesses of a follower. For example, if you do not like an employee very much and then learn that s/he was drunk at an after-work happy hour, you could use this to really hurt the employee on the job by spreading the story. This is unacceptable. Leadership has limits.

Leaders Know They Cannot Have It All

જાર્જી

Choices have to be made. In a corporate budget, new buildings may mean fewer products to sell. Married people cannot lead a single lifestyle, and single people do not have the joys of marriage. Athletes do not enjoy junk food. When visiting another land, tourists must accept the ways of its people and government as legitimate even if they do not agree. *Life is a trade off, and a leader knows it!*

Leadership Has Become Endangered under the Weight of and the Preoccupation with Management

જાર્જી

As stated earlier, management is important and necessary; but it is not all that is needed to have a successful organization, family, or nation.

When invited to keynote a national conference for one of the major departments of the federal government, I was asked to speak on Total Quality Management (TQM). Any student of management is aware of Deming's work in TQM and his important help to Japan's restructuring after World War II. It is really quite good stuff and is still a beneficial process to help improve organizational management today. To make my point, I agreed to title my talk "TQM Is Useless Without Leadership." This was no reflection on TQM and, of course, a stretch; but it was an attempt to expand the focus of an important government agency about governance. "Dare To Be A Leader" was the final title for this talk. I think a few heard me.

For many years in our firm, we had one of the finest accounts receivable managers in the office-technology business – efficient, capable, dedicated, focused, fair, and loyal. Few, however, would have considered him one of our corporate leaders. He would be the first to say he was proud to be just the accounts receivable manager. He supervised a few associates and managed an activity about "stuff" few knew so well, but to ask him to be a corporate leader was more than he wanted.

The danger in the previous story is that many organizations are so preoccupied with this organizational skill of management that they do not see the other need employees have, the need to be led. We would not have traded our accounts receivable manager for anyone. We honored his management skill and appreciated his contribution as a manager, but we could not force him to provide wide corporate leadership as I will define it herein.

Leadership and management are not synonymous, and you cannot expect or demand leadership from those who manage well. Maybe they can lead; maybe they cannot. Maybe they want to lead, maybe they do not.

Leadership Is about Being a Servant
ॐॐ

Leadership is a one-way street. Don't kid yourself. A leader must have the conviction, commitment, and moral and mental strength *to give* most of the time. This is not a reciprocal relationship, like a marriage or a friendship. *When you set yourself apart to lead, you must be prepared to give much and to give up much.*

This also suggests that leaders cannot be selfish and ambitious at the expense of others. They must be willing to let others pass them by. Better said, leaders take their greatest joy in those who go *beyond* them in an endeavor of life. While many would not agree, what other motive can servants have but to see others expand, develop, and move past them? Without this motive, what hope for the future is there for any organization, family, group, or nation?

This is an area in which many struggle because of the notion in our culture that we should try hard, compete, and be the best. The idea of being a leader/servant is not inconsistent with this; rather, it is a willingness to see others do as well or even *better* as a reward in itself. Am I setting too high a standard? I hope so, for leadership is a high standard.

I could spend the rest of this book telling you about individuals that I have been privileged to lead who have passed me by. I sincerely take joy in seeing former students and employees achieve greater distinction in society than I have achieved. (I hope all of us feel that way about our own children and the young people we influence.) I dare not say anymore, for it might go to their heads.

Leadership Demands Inclusion and Reconciliation
જ∽ઈ

Good leadership might be one of the best strategies for including diverse people in an organization or effort. Leaders are not as interested in color, creed, or orientation as they are in finding the highest common denominator between and among peoples and cultures upon which to hang a solution. The leader is always interested in bringing reconciliation, not in creating polarization, between and among peoples and groups.

One of the great sadnesses in my one brief experience in politics is that politics often forces people to anger 45% of the voting population in order to attract the other 55% of the population needed to win. We ought to find individuals who are skilled and who are committed to bringing people together. Is this idealistic? I suppose so, but it is also necessary to be a leader.

Reconciliation is very difficult. During one of my visits to the Middle East, I had a number of focused discussions with several Israeli and Arab colleagues and friends. To summarize the majority opinion of these colleagues, they felt they were a *long way* from settlement in that region because it is so rooted in religious and cultural beliefs, experiences, and norms.

A few months after I returned from this visit, I was invited to give a lecture on diversity for the leadership of a corporation. I suggested that better leadership (inclusion and reconciliation) was as legitimate a strategy for addressing diversity as training.

Please do not misquote me. Training in all issues, including diversity, is important; but few consider better leadership as another way. I find less religious, ethnic, and gender difficulty in organizations, families, cities, or other units where there is really good leadership. This is because leaders are focused on finding *talent* to accomplish the mission, and they know they must look in *every segment of society* to find it.

The goal of a leader must be inclusion and reconciliation; and the tougher the issues become, the more inclusive and reconciling a leader must be.

Here is another point to consider about inclusion: Closed doors worry people. Seldom do I close my door. When I do, it is done with caution because it makes employees feel excluded. While this may seem insignificant, it is not.

Litigiousness Often Dims Leadership

কৈল্ড

I will be in a pack of trouble on this comment, but I ask the reader to consider objectively what I say. No one is more proud of the laws that govern our American society and our commercial life than I am, and I would have it no other way in resolving irresolvable issues. Yet, having said this, I must suggest that leaders always search for ways other than the legal system to resolve differences and issues – good will, new and better understandings, communication, and good faith. Otherwise, we can create more ill will than a successful organization can endure. I am not referring to an individual's right to sue for his/her rights. I am speaking only to leaders. A lawsuit seldom brings people together. Practice leadership; it helps.

As a kid, I remember adults saying, "It's okay to make mistakes; that is how you learn." Now, we often hear, "Cover your butt."

Today, any mistake could result in a legal suit. I am sorry to say that people – teachers, bus drivers, doctors, accountants, etc. – do and always will make mistakes. I am afraid that if all a leader does is protect him/herself from legal procedures s/he will not always be practicing the best leadership.

Some years ago, when I first joined my brother with our company, I helped write a policy called Fun and Fellowship Day. It was a day designed to give employees an extra day off and to encourage them to have fun (see a movie, tour a museum, go white water rafting) with other colleagues from work and their families. For years our employees loved this special day.

One year a group chose jeeping. In a terrible tragedy, the jeep turned over. A wonderful employee was killed, as was a son of one of our other special employees. It was one of the worst days of my life with the company.

The ones who survived did everything right, for they are wonderful people. Yet, without going into detail here, one of the insurance claims suggested that Lloyd Lewan created a zone of danger, which resulted in a tragedy, only because I helped write the policy and the company benefited from this special vacation day. I will never forget this incident. It was resolved amicably, but you get the point.

I realize how this sounds, but many legal cases give very little room for honest mistakes and for doing your best. I am not saying I am totally on target here; but, when considering leadership, you need to really think about this.

Leadership Is a Relationship, Not a Role
ॐॐ

In an article in *Fortune*, June 21, 1999, by R. Charan and Geoffrey Colvin, entitled "Why CEO's Fail," they say, "The motto of successful CEO's: People first, strategy second."

Leadership is a proper and professional relationship you have with others; it is not a stance or a role you fill for them. You must know who your follower is to properly lead him/her. If it is a large group, then you must have a serious relationship with the group so you know what is important.

Leadership is very personal. I found a sticker, a little white piece of paper, in one of my new suits. It read, "Inspected by Inspector #175." Why couldn't it have read, "Inspected by Sally S., #175, Detroit, Michigan. Feel free to leave her a message

about the quality of the suit at 1-800-888-SUIT"?
You know what I mean by this story. Leadership is
becoming a *person* to those you serve.

When sailing with Semester at Sea and when
working in my own firm, I learn names, write
birthday notes, and discover all I am able about as
many as I can.

When you add up the sum total of leadership
in an organization, at least *one* leader should know a
lot about each and every person. It makes a difference
to those who follow.

Opening a textbook on management, I read
the first sentence: "The *role* of management is to..."
(italics added). I know what the author meant, and it
is perfectly fine to open this way. I do not mean to be
petty. Yet, I am trying to suggest that a book on
leadership should begin: "The *responsibility* and the
commitment of a leader is to...." This distinction
seems so insignificant on the surface, but it is not.

Some years ago I wrote a book entitled *Women
in the Workplace: A Man's Perspective*. To summarize
very briefly, I said that women generally have a
natural and greater appreciation for relationship than

men do. In his book *The Magus*, John Fowles stated it this way: Men see objects; women see the relationships between objects.

If leadership is a relationship, as I believe it is, women, raise your hands to indicate you are interested in leadership. Often, you hesitate because you think you are not quite prepared or you first want to be perfect at what you do. Forget it. If you want to lead and you have the passion and the commitment to care and to sacrifice, then *raise your hands*. (We men have been doing so for years and not quite prepared either.)

Leadership is developed, but you must *first* have the willingness and the commitment. *We need leaders now — men and women!*

Leadership transcends gender and race. If organizations could separate their thinking about leadership and management, women and other minorities would fare better.

Leadership Is Not about Talent – It Is about Freeing Talent

ॐॐ

Many believe that leadership is about the leader's talent. It is actually more about freeing the talent of those who follow. This is not to suggest that leadership and talent do not go together, but an important responsibility as a leader is to free talent.

When you are able to attract a fine group of professionals in an organization, it seems to work best if you can create a large "corral" for these "thoroughbreds" so they can interact. Although they might kick up some dust, to place really great people in individual "stalls" reduces the synergy, the competition, and the respect that grows among serious professionals. To make this work, however, requires good leadership because strong people are easier to "box up" if you want to restrict them.

Lao Tzu's *Tao Te Ching*, one of China's best books of wisdom, suggests that it is not so much what a leader gets done but what gets done under his/her watch. This is offered as a red flag to those who always claim to be too busy. Selflessness is about freeing others.

Our job as leaders is to free talent. It always has been, and it always will be.

Leadership Failure Is Not Always the Leader's Fault

෧෬

All employees must be touched by good leadership and good management. These, however, are not always embodied in the same person. The best certified public accountant does not necessarily make the firm's best managing partner; the best leader does. The best trial attorney does not always make the best firm leader; the best leader does. The best salesperson does not always make the best sales leader; the best leader does. The better faculty members are not always the best candidates for university presidents; the best leaders are. Therefore, how can we find the best leaders if we have not spent the time deciding what leadership really is?

A colleague of mine was appointed to the presidency of a large university as a compromise candidate. It was a difficult few years for this person. Eventually, the person was asked to leave.

The faculty had one agenda for the president; the deans and the administration, another; the alumni and students had their set of priorities. Finally, the governing board had still another idea of what the university president should provide. This president was like a horse, with four ropes tied to its four legs, being pulled by four strong persons in four opposing directions. To win was impossible.

Many looked to the president to assign blame; yet, as much blame needed to be focused on the university since it was the institution that appointed this individual to the position. Although a part of the problem was mismatching, the institution placed total blame on the leader.

Know what you want and need in a leader before you go looking. Many organizations go for an opposite skill set when they are unhappy with their present leadership. That usually does not work for long either.

Simply, we must know what leadership is, does, and provides before we go looking for a leader. Otherwise, the person selected has a dismal chance of long-term success or survival.

We must also be conscious of when change occurs in our organizations. We expect leaders to always adjust, but we fail to remember that we hired them at a time when we believed "A." When change happens, we expect them to be our new "Z." We must help them change, too.

Leadership Is Not a Calling for Victims or a Platform for Personal Agendas

৵৽

If you feel you have been wronged or your number one mission in life is to right your wrong, it will be difficult for you to lead, except in a group dedicated to your cause.

Righting a wrong may be very important, but a leader's personal agenda to do so must not become of greater importance than the defined mission of the corporation/organization. I heard a senior official in the department of energy say, "My number one goal is to bring diversity to this agency." I cannot quarrel with diversity as an important goal; but anyone responsible for energy must *first* concentrate on inexpensive, continuous, deliverable energy for the people the department serves.

I heard another well-known activist in America say recently, "My number one goal is to get the republicans out of office." If this is truly the goal, then it is virtually impossible for this person to lead a republican. This is a right in a free society, but it limits leadership.

Sadly, in America it is often easier to get government action if you can create some form of victimization for yourself. I finally found a victims' group to which I can belong – those opposed to undersized and cramped airline seats. That's me – 250 pounds at least.

Do not misread me. Many wrongs in America need correction; but leaders must rise above most of them to keep their objectivity, their perspective, and their sense of fairness to all in order to see that the mission is accomplished.

Leadership Is about Hope
ॐ∾

Napoleon Bonaparte (1769-1821), Emperor of France, said, "No person can lead other people except by showing them a future. A leader is a merchant of hope."

Arthur C. Clarke, the noted writer, scholar, and futurist, is a friend. In a postcard he sent me a while ago, the caption written by him simply says: "The universe is such a strange and wonderful place that reality will always out run the wildest imagination; there will always be things unknown, and perhaps unknowable." Leadership brings hope.

Leadership Requires an Appreciative Spirit
დ◆

In the heart of a leader is an appreciative spirit, especially toward those who follow.

I must stop here and give my sister-in-law, Marjorie, credit. She is the one who introduced me to this idea of an appreciative spirit as she always tells me how appreciative she is for her life, her husband, her children, her family, and her faith.

Asked to give a keynote address sometime ago on leadership, I thought I would entitle it "Is your Toilet Paper Soft?" (I almost titled this book that way.) As I wrote the speech, I described the many kinds of toilet paper that I find in my local grocery store – four ply, extra soft, quilted. My point, of course, is that we are so fortunate in this country because we have so much and so many choices. Many on earth have no toilet paper, and many who do have some pretty rough stuff.

On the day I wrote this paragraph, I woke up healthy, relaxed under a hot shower, ate three great meals at whatever time I wanted, used a flushing indoor toilet, enjoyed a nice work day, interacted with wonderful colleagues, came home to many electronic and material amenities, and walked to a university library where I am free to write and to think anything I want. Am I appreciative? YES! I am so very appreciative.

As leaders we must do our work with an appreciative spirit, appreciative of the work we have been given and of the freedoms we enjoy.

My brother and I are so very appreciative of the hundreds of employees who have made our company successful. We could never have done it without them.

It is simply impossible for a leader to give all that is asked without this appreciative spirit. This is not to say that a leader cannot feel victimized, unappreciated, frustrated, or angered or that having these feelings is wrong; but, for those who want to lead, shake them out, deal with them, and get past them. Otherwise, leadership will be tainted. *I repeat, at the heart of a leader is an appreciative spirit.*

Enough background. Let me now move your thinking to the definition of leadership.

PART II

LEADERSHIP

THE NOTIONS
OF LEADERSHIP

⫽ VISION

To lead, you must be the number one
believer in a realistic mission that can
be embraced by your followers. Only
then can you excite your followers to
action.

⫽ FOCUS

To lead, you must keep followers
focused on what is important to
ensure that the job is done, that the
mission is accomplished, or that the
family is strong.

⫽ INFLUENCE

To lead, you must earn the trust of
your followers through your sincere
motive and consistent behavior.

Chapter Six

VISION:
THE FIRST
RESPONSIBILITY
OF LEADERSHIP

Vision:
The First Responsibility
of Leadership

In the simplest of terms, if you want others to follow you, you must turn them on and then keep them excited about the mission, about what you have agreed to do together. This is vision, the first responsibility of leadership.

To best understand this notion, it is helpful to break it into two parts. First, you have to be *the number one believer* in what you do; and, second, this belief *must be realistic.*

Belief

As a leader you cannot convey a vision, a mission, or a goal that will excite others unless, honestly, *you are the number one believer.* You must be a believer and show it to lead. If you are faking it, your followers will surely find you out. You must demonstrate consistently that you believe, above all others, in the organization (or in the mission) and in its people.

The best teachers I had all through school were not the ones who were necessarily easy and fun. Rather, they were those who believed so much in what they taught that I began to catch on. Their excitement about the subject matter soon became my excitement about the subject matter.

My brother, Paul, founded our company and was the leader because *he* was the number one believer. Many others and I have heard him say, "We are in the right industry, at the right time, in the right region of the country, with the right people." He believes this to this day.

He could really become excited about a new product that served customers, provided good commissions for the sales force, resulted in future supplies and service, and returned a fair profit to the company. Can you just see that excitement on his face (or the faces of others you know who are successful)?

We have a number of senior officers in our corporation, and my brother met with the same executive on the same day of the week for years at our executive dining room – the local Arby's near our office. What was my brother doing? He was keeping in close touch and always "dipping" each of his key persons in the company belief system. It took us years to realize the value of this special time with these key leaders in our company.

Every Disney employee must attend a lecture called "Traditions I" at Disney University before starting employment at Disneyland or Disney World. Traditions I at Disney is no different than my brother starting each morning at Arby's with his senior executives to keep them united in the Lewan & Associates' belief system.

My doctoral dissertation led me to one clear objective finding: In a successful organization, internal congruence of belief is more important than the actual belief. The common thread in a successful organization is the common belief. In great organizations the key leaders, at least, share a common belief about how to lead, to run, to organize, and to administer an organization. Different personalities and different talents are needed, but common belief or mission is essential to success.

I am old enough to remember Dr. Martin Luther King standing in Washington on the steps of the Washington Monument on August 28, 1963. He did not stand and say, "I have twenty-three objectives in behavioral terms that I want to promulgate in memo form for your consideration." He said, "Deep in my heart, I do believe....I have a dream." His influence is still with us. Certainly, he was the acknowledged number one believer in the civil-rights movement in our nation; and he deserves the title of believer/leader whether or not you agreed with him.

Some years ago I had a meal with a distinguished judge. During the meal he complained to me about the entire judicial system – plea bargaining, mandatory sentencing, district attorneys, police officers, red tape, pressure, and the growing apathy of young people who came before his bench. After a really fine meal and after he had paid for the meal, my simple advice to him as we left the restaurant was, "Resign your bench." He responded, "After I pay, that's your advice?"

He does not believe anymore in the sanctity of our judicial system, however imperfect and in need of improvement it may be. I would be reluctant to come before him to have my indiscretions judged, for his "prejudices" became clear to me. To have faith in the judicial process, I must assume that he believes in what he does for me, a simple citizen. I want to have my mistakes judged as objectively in the courtroom as possible. Certainly, he has the right to fight for what he believes needs to be changed and to express occasional disappointment; but I would expect a judge, with his awesome power and responsibility, to interpret the law, to be a firm believer in the fundamental system he represents, and to show it to all who touch him.

In contrast to the previous situation, I recently served as a jury foreman. Very objective in her comments and thoughtful in her dealings, the judge briefed the jury without bias or frustration. I was impressed, for I felt that she truly believed in the process. What an example of good leadership.

Don't we all like to visit restaurants where the chef is the number one believer? It usually results in a better meal. Isn't this equally true in our houses of religious worship? Everyone would like to believe that the person in the pulpit is the number one believer. When it is not so, the organization is less likely to attract others.

Invited years ago by the chancellor of the University of Arkansas, Little Rock, to address his collective faculty on leadership, I suggested that, in addition to teaching, faculty should be responsible for the *retention* of students in some way. This would require an *excitement* for and a *belief* in their discipline to attract students. In essence, this would be a part of their leadership on behalf of the university.

As mentioned at the beginning of this book, I have been affiliated for nearly thirty-five years with Semester at Sea, a program of international study conducted by The Institute of Shipboard Education. Over the years I have been privileged to work with their dedicated administrative staff and to serve on board ship as the executive dean taking students, adults, faculty, and staff on voyages around the world. While some would say that I am not the best executive dean in the world, most would agree that I am among the top *believers* in this program.

Many international educators have argued that the value of Semester at Sea is limited because it is not an immersion (focused on one country) program, but we have discovered that it is an excellent comparative and introductory *prelude* to the rest of our students' lives because we live in an increasingly interdependent world. For example, consider our large urban centers today. We see the beginning of the "third world" (the growing alienation of the have's and the have not's) creeping in. An underclass is growing in America, and we have to see this in other parts of the world to understand. Therefore, I am a firm *believer* in what Semester at Sea has provided for these many years.

Quite a few years ago, when interviewing for the top position in a liberal arts college, I was asked what one thing I would require of the college if I were selected. Without hesitation, because of my experience with the Semester at Sea program, I responded, "I would not grant a bachelor's degree to a single student who had not at least traveled somewhere in the third world." Students cannot live fully in an interdependent world, especially one so divided by have's and have not's, until they have had a beginning introduction to the third world. (They did not offer me the job.)

Realism

The second part of vision and the companion idea to being the number one believer is *realism*. Your mission, job expectations, and excitement have to be realistic; or they will be perceived as fluff or pie in the sky. Fluff and pie in the sky help no one to follow. They only lead to disappointment.

One of my favorite writers on leadership is Max Dupree. In his early work, *Leadership is an Art*, he defined leadership along these lines:

> The first responsibility of a leader is to define reality. The last is to say thank you. In between the two, the leader must become a servant....That sums up the progress of an artful leader.

Most hear the thank you and the servant part, but few hear the reality part. If you want to lead, you *must create a dream that all can embrace; but you must also make sure that it is rooted in reality.*

A clear example of an unrealistic resume for employment was received one day. The cover letter stated: "Do you want a man who turned a 250K loss into a 157K profit?" Being a businessman, I realize that this could happen, but only with many people helping. For one person to claim that this was his accomplishment is self-serving at the least. Be real when you write your resume, please. Facts, jobs, beliefs, and interests are what reviewers want to see, not a lot of fluff and inflated claims. This also applies to leadership. Be realistic, not fluffy.

Let me give you another example. The mission statement for a college at which I was invited to give the commencement address states: "The mission of X University is to provide personalized education of distinction that leads to inquiring, ethical, and productive lives as global citizens." The university means well and, in fact, probably does a little of this some of the time. Yet, as fewer than five percent of its students travel abroad, this claim of global citizenship might be a little overstated. I agree with the aim, but it is going to take much more of a commitment to accomplish with any certainty or regularity.

So many wonderful, articulate, and well-meaning organizational mission statements have been written over the years. You probably have one for your workplace. Yet, I wonder if many of these are not really written as public-relations statements for public consumption.

My point is not to criticize. Rather, it is to ask those interested in leadership to tailor their mission statements so that they excite those who work for the organization/institution. Keep them simple, attainable, and believable. Perhaps a better mission statement for the university noted previously would be: "We take high-school talent, attempt to show these students how to learn, to think critically and objectively, to find information, to begin to think about what is important, and to prepare for employment in our society." While this is not good public relations, it is honest and realistic.

This may raise some eyebrows, but think about it. Public relations is important, even legitimate; but, to those who serve as participants and as workers, in their eyes, the mission statement must be realistic and attainable.

I am the chairman of the board for a not-for-profit program focused on deterring young people, particularly urban youth, from being enticed into gangs or into other violent behaviors. We had to greatly reduce our mission statement to one we could manage and achieve, potential donors would believe in, and volunteers could embrace. Our focus was so complicated in the beginning: mediating among gangs and community leaders; working with police; interfacing with older gang members; educating young, potential gang members. Many people in the community were suspicious of us. We decided to come up with a realistic statement to focus the program.

Now, all we do is measured against this simple goal: "To help elementary school children in select public schools in Denver, Colorado, resist gang-recruitment activities and approaches by providing special programs, study opportunities, athletics, and food after school until their parents arrive at home." Because crime and gang recruitment are high between 2 p.m. and 5 p.m. daily, our main programs are alternative activities and tutoring sessions after school and during school vacations. We are invited by and work with school administrations. It is a very exciting program under the *leadership* of Reverend

Leon Kelly. We are making a difference, and we are very realistic.

My interest in and commitment to work with urban youth across all cultures come from my sincere belief, gained by my many years of international travel, in the following two realizations:

◆ Most violence in culture is male initiated. Therefore, one of society's objectives should be to put a man, a moral man, in the life of every boy through any method. Women are faithful; and, of course, boys need women. Yet, to thwart violence, a boy needs a man to model moral and acceptable behavior.

◆ How go America's cities goes America. The issues facing our large urban centers – education, poverty, cultural unrest, alienation, housing, jobs – must be addressed for us to remain a great nation.

Realism showed up in a poster designed by Thomas and Perkins in Colorado to keep kids focused on the dangers and on the direction of gang violent behaviors. The poster shows six young people carrying a coffin. The caption reads: "Join a gang. You'll have plenty of friends to give you a lift when you need it." What is my point? All we do as leaders to excite people must be grounded in realism.

Being in business for many years, I have, of course, been involved in the hiring process. When asked what types of jobs we have open in our office-technology dealership, I usually start with, "You are either recruiting a customer or retaining one. There are no other jobs." This may sound flippant to some; but it is what I believe, and it is realistic. If you are a customer-service representative, a copier technician or a systems technician, you are in the retention business. If you sell, you are in the recruitment business. Our employees generally respond to the characterization.

Somewhere I read, "Sales is courtship; service is marriage." This statement is believable and realistic to anyone in business. It expresses a clear vision – the first responsibility of a leader.

A large AAA affiliate of the Automobile Association of America invited me to give a keynote address. A great service organization, AAA runs well because they offer a great product. I have been a happy member for many years. They asked me to speak about leadership; and, by now, you know this is my favorite subject. I asked to see their mission statement. It was okay – a little long, not overly exciting, and, again, more of a public-relations statement than something the employees could get excited about. During my talk I suggested a new mission statement for the employees: "Next to *National Geographic*, AAA is the best buy in America – forty-five dollars, multiple tows, recovered keys, and a few maps – and all with a smile." Perhaps it was not exactly accurate, but it was close enough to make the point. I was visiting some weeks later; one of their employees had it written on a post-it note above his desk.

A few years ago, the University of Phoenix, the largest private university in America, invited me to deliver their commencement address in Denver. Many of my colleagues in higher education do not agree with the University of Phoenix' for-profit concept or its way of conducting higher education. Yet, from my point of view, they are honest about what they offer and provide a good service. Before I agreed to do the commencement, I read their brochure and talked to a number of graduates. The opening statement in the piece of literature I had stated, "We help working adults earn their degrees...." That impressed me. It was forthright, clear, not misleading, and, most importantly, realistic.

⊱⊰

Show me a church filled with kids; I'll show you a theologian/leader in the pulpit. Show me a restaurant with a crowd waiting; I'll show you a chef/leader in the kitchen. Show me a class always over-enrolled; I'll show you a teacher/leader in the classroom. Show me a good family, I'll show you parents/leaders in the home.

The first responsibility of a leader is vision – show it, articulate it, believe it, and keep it real. In this a leader cannot waiver.

Chapter Seven

FOCUS:
THE SECOND
RESPONSIBILITY
OF LEADERSHIP

Focus:
The Second Responsibility
of Leadership

On one of my voyages with Semester at Sea, the students were a bit "antsy;" and they brought to my attention a list of issues – pits in the cherry pie, foam pillows, lumpy mattresses, inconsistent air conditioning, and unexpected changes in shower water temperature, to mention a few. It was "that time" in the voyage.

The students asked for a town-hall meeting; it was scheduled for early one Saturday evening. Entering the crowded student union, I was presented with this list of concerns. Students were invited to add to "the list." I listened carefully, took notes, and left the meeting, agreeing to look into each item in my notes and on their list.

Following me, when I left, was the student moderator. He stopped me as I was going into my office to sort through the list of issues. He said, "You need to say something to the students."

I mentioned to him that I had nothing to say, for I understood their concerns. Nevertheless, he insisted. Because of his urging, I returned to the student union. Microphone in hand, I looked into the eyes of a good number of students and then softly spoke six words: *"China tomorrow, China tomorrow, China tomorrow."*

The ship was due to dock in Hong Kong for our visit to the People's Republic of China the next morning; and, after all, the Semester at Sea program is designed to introduce students to the cultures and the countries that do and would influence their lives and the lives of their children. As the leader it was my responsibility and charge to keep the students focused on our primary mission, regardless of the side issues that had now become so nagging and annoying.

Life has numerous distractions, many of which are unavoidable; and leaders must keep followers "out of the weeds" and focused on what counts.

This is focus, the second responsibility of a leader: helping followers grasp what is really important and constantly bringing them back to the source, the heart, the important issues in order to accomplish the mission or to achieve the goal.

While president and CEO of Lewan & Associates, my brother always did what was important. We are a sales and service organization in office technology, and my brother knew what was priority. He wasn't worrying about the wallpaper in the bathrooms or the oil spots in the parking lot – just what we were doing for our customers.

For years I watched him sit at his desk and look through the "goldenrods," copies of our invoices for each sale. From these he could tell the product, the customer, the size of the deal, the commission to be paid, and a number of other important details about each sale. On ever so many of these invoices, he wrote a note to the salesperson;

or he called customers noted on the invoices to thank them for their business.

A salesperson could not pass him in the hall without his asking excitedly, "What do you have going this month?" He really wanted to know and concluded with, "I'm proud of you."

In addition, he writes an anniversary letter to each of our employees on the month of his/her work anniversary, making special comments about that person and offering greetings to the family members. Our employees treasure these letters.

Of course, he was engaged in corporate decision-making and strategic issues; but he was always focused on what was important to our company – our customers and our associates.

A leader makes sense of the mission, and this involves prioritizing and seeing the final piece.

Secretary of State, retired General Colin Powell said, "Great leaders are almost always great simplifiers who can cut through argument, debate and doubt to offer a solution everybody can understand."

If there is a fire, you must lean your ladder against the right building. Leaders find the right issues and then stay focused on them.

I don't remember who said this, but I know it was a baseball quote. "Don't major in the minors." If you know what is really important, the job or the mission is more likely to be completed well.

One of my regimens is to walk a few miles each day; and one of my favorite walking spots is a tree-lined, beautiful cemetery near my home. After a few visits to this particular cemetery (and bored with walking), I started to read gravestones. Having done this for a number of days, it struck me: I never saw "VP Finance," "MBA," "Full Professor," or "CEO" on any of these grave markers. Mostly, I found endearments such as, "Devoted Father," "My best friend," "Beloved Mom," and "Our treasured daughter." I also noticed that those proud of their service to the country they loved referenced their military service on their markers. What is important is usually found on a gravestone.

Some time ago I was invited to participate in the memorial service of a man who was very important in my life, Dr. Wilfred Landrus. He was my first leader in my academic career at Chapman University in California. Dr. Robert Schuller was conducting the service at the Crystal Cathedral in Garden Grove, California. As I prepared for my small part in this service, I spoke with his wife, my friend Clara, and asked what his last days were like.

She told me that he had not spoken a word in months due to Parkinson's disease. One evening, while sitting in their home near the final day of his life, she asked him, "What should I put on your final resting marker?" Slowly, he responded with words for the first time in a long time. To her surprise and delight, he said, "Put 'I loved my wife.'" After the tears cleared my eyes, I knew how serious it is for a leader to know and to stay focused on what is really important.

These events are constant reminders as to what is really important in life, and leaders must stay focused on life's larger, important issues. In doing so, however, they must not overlook the small areas of life.

As a sales organization, our company operates from a number of simple sales principles we consider important. Here are two to make my point:

☑ *Show up.*
You need to be in front of a customer to sell anything.

☑ *STP – See twenty people a day*
Sales is a business of averages. If you do the drill day in and day out, it will eventually result in sales.

Over the years I have learned that it is not always easy to identify what is important or sacred to those you serve; but, if your goal is to be a good leader, you must discover what is important or sacred to them. You need to understand their needs so you can better fit those you serve to the mission.

For example, when students, faculty, staff, employees, or colleagues come to me as their leader, I have learned that I first must find out what it is they want. Before any interaction I ask myself these questions:

Does this person want me
- to simply listen?
- to make a decision?
- to provide information or guidance?

- to give my opinion or perspective so s/he might go back and do it better for him/herself?

If I give advice when the follower wants me merely to listen, I fail. If I give a decision when the follower only wants advice, I also fail.

Leaders must also know what is important/sacred in *their* lives, for how can they focus others if they are not focused themselves?

In a very difficult transition in my life, I was struggling a great deal. After one of my walks in that favorite cemetery, I decided to write what I would like people to remember about me at the end of my life. I hope that those I have served and loved will say...

- He was peaceful.
- He was a full participant in life.
- He was a follower as well as a leader.
- He loved and was loved.
- He gave without notice.
- He was a man of faith.

Times will come when you lose focus as a leader and your strength to lead fades. Leadership duties press heavily, discouragement creeps in, and beliefs wane. When this happens, use symbols to keep going. I do. Symbols make it easier to lead. Consider these four fun symbols:

ଔ The "boot"
   – to keep your sense of humor.

ଔ The "baton"
   – to make sure you notice what counts.

ଔ The "X"
   – to admit you are "not in service."

ଔ "Straight scoop"
   – a commitment to share honestly with those you serve.

The "boot" came to me while serving with the United States Marine Corps. I was to be the commanding officer of troops for a parade to honor Speaker of the House Sam Rayburn and the late President John F. Kennedy. They did not show, but someone important did.

I did not have my sword for the parade, so I borrowed one from a tall friend (6'4"). This was a bit risky because a marine's sword is sized to come to the center of the ear when holding it at the side of the body. Therefore, my friend's sword came way above my ear, for I am only six-feet tall, at best. When marching by the dignitaries, I raised the sword to my nose, looked right, and ordered, "Eyes right." I then brought the sword down at an angle of forty-five degrees to my front. As it was too long for me, it hit the asphalt, flew out of my hand, and hit the private in the first row of troops. Trying to look normal, I raised my hand in a salute and kept marching. When later introduced to the dignitaries, one who saw it all commented, "Nice recovery, Captain." I responded, "Thank you, Sir."

My fellow officers awarded me "the boot" for the blunder – a real Marine Corps boot, painted gold and filled with concrete, to carry around with me for the next week.

Now, on all my voyages of Semester at Sea, I give boots to keep our collective sense of humor. For example, a student came rushing into the dining room, bumped into a four-way floor-to-ceiling mirror in the center of the room and, without thinking, said to his own reflection, "Oh, excuse me." He got the boot.

The "baton" is a symbol I also started using on the ship many years ago. When I observe a student or a faculty or staff member doing something special or thoughtful (an act that was unsolicited, kind, and unnoticed) for another on board the ship, I extend to that person a symbolic baton. This person usually asks what I saw; and, of course, I do not tell. It is obvious that the person appreciates that I noticed, and not knowing what s/he did encourages *more* thoughtful behavior.

The third symbol for illustrative purposes is the "X." I ask anyone who is having a tough, stressful, or difficult day to put an X on his/her forehead. What's the point? It tells others on the ship that this person admits that today is not that good. It shows s/he is human, and it takes the heat off others to figure out what is wrong. It changes the behavior of friends, colleagues, and followers toward this person. S/he will probably get a few more hugs, a few more thoughtful looks, and a wide array of other "niceties."

"Straight Scoop" is another favorite of mine. The idea came to me when I was on the television show "To Tell the Truth" many years ago as the dean for World Campus Afloat. These two words I give to students as a gift early in the voyage. I ask them not to use these words unless something is really getting to them and they are frightened, nervous, or in some other way upset. If they preface any question to me with "Straight Scoop," they can count on a straight answer. If I cannot tell them, I will say that.

- ☐ One student came to me and asked as we approached Florida, "Straight Scoop: Is it safe for us to go through the Bermuda Triangle?" She was serious.

- ■ I responded with, "Yes," no further editorial comment, just, yes.

- ☐ "Straight Scoop: Dean, are we going to change the itinerary because the *U.S.S. Cole* was blown up in the Suez Canal?"

- ■ My response, "I am not sure yet, but probably. The moment we decide, I will announce it."

☐ Knowing that he had been drinking excessively and that I had been watching, a student asked, "Straight Scoop: Are you happy with my behavior, Dean?"

■ "No, I am a little disappointed, knowing what kind of person you really are."

A reminder: Straight Scoop, as with all honesty, is always offered with kindness. I do not offer any more than what the students ask for. If they want more, it is their right to ask for more. That is part of the Straight Scoop – an honest answer upon which they can do something, say something, or ask something, or just drop it with no repercussion.

Symbolism helps keep all *focused* on your leadership. Make up your own. They are fun.

Chapter Eight

INFLUENCE:
THE KEY INGREDIENT
OF LEADERSHIP

TEN COMMANDMENTS
OF INFLUENCE

ॐॐ

- Value people genuinely and make sure they know it.

- Separate behavior from worth.

- Speak in your own voice.

- Seek an improved batting average, not perfection or comparison with others.

- Spend as much time on the *how* and on the *when* as on the *what*.

- Demonstrate grace under pressure.

- Fire people or help people.

- Listen to people.

- Keep your eye on the faithful.

- Help people gain perspective and context for their work, mission, lives, and messes.

Influence:
The Key Ingredient
of Leadership

People often ask me if Adolph Hitler, Joseph Stalin, Sadam Hussein, Idi Amin, or Pol Pot were leaders. *No.* Even though they moved people to action and were focused in their aims, they were not leaders; they were despots.

Influence, this third aspect of leadership, is the *defining characteristic* of a leader. You will not gain positive influence over your followers *unless* your *motive* toward them is *pure*.

If ordered, people will do as they are told; but they will not freely give a person influence over them unless they trust that person's motive. *Motive separates the true leader from all others who so easily claim the title of leader.*

It is human to search for motive, to even suspect it. Not too long ago, I spoke to a large group of women. During the talk, I asked this question: "Would you join me in Vail for the weekend?" Then I asked, "What first went through your mind when you heard the question?" Just about every woman raised her hand when I suggested that they were concerned about my motive.

When Latin Americans or African-Americans hear Caucasians talking about how much they enjoy people of color, the minority has to ask, "What is the motive for that statement?"

Men who exclaim they appreciate women are suspect until proven otherwise. When I wrote the book, *Women in the Workplace: A Man's Perspective*, did I catch it from some! What was my motive for writing this?

If only we could read another's motive easily. We would make fewer bad decisions, and life would be simpler. But, we cannot. We can only guess at motive by the way we are treated by others.

Therefore, it is critical that you give those who follow you a sense, a glimpse, an idea of your motive by the way you treat them. *This is the only way they can ascertain what your motive is toward them, and only when they trust your motive will they give you influence over them.*

Of course, it is clearly implied that to demonstrate a pure motive, your motive must indeed *be* pure. Your actions must show that within human ability you want the best for the individuals and the organizations you serve. As a leader you must reach inside to examine your motive toward your followers If you fake it, your followers will eventually see through you.

The following ten commandments *or principles* of influence will tell you if your motives are pure. I have selected these behaviors because my experiences as a follower and as a leader have taught me that these ten give the best clues about motive.

ONE:
Value people genuinely
and make sure they know it.

೪೦೯

Simply, that which you cannot value, you cannot lead, understand, communicate with, or team with. Followers are less able to trust your motive if they suspect you do not value them. Therefore, you must find a legitimate way to value them and to assure them that you value them, genuinely.

Asked to conduct a seminar on team building for an organization, I immediately paired up the participants and sent them out to spend time together. They were to return with only one requirement – to introduce, as fully as possible, their teammates. When each pair returned and after they shared introductions, I had them pair differently. We repeated the activity, again and again. What was my point? There is no sense in creating a team unless each member sees value in the other members. This can be accomplished in many ways, but the first requirement is to *want to value another*.

The founder of Mary Kay Cosmetics, the late Mary Kay Ash, represented one of America's great success stories. She did many things right, and among them was valuing people a great deal. I see enough pink Cadillacs on the streets to prove that! Recognition was what she always gave so freely. At her sales rallies she hugged, patted hands, put roses in laps, looked deeply into eyes, and listened carefully. She valued by showing deep respect for each employee.

The governor of Colorado appointed me to a number of terms on the Women's Economic Development Council for Colorado. Often, I was the token male at the meetings. This was a very good experience for me. I was always a little nervous to offer an opinion, to argue, or to make a suggestion because the women appointed to the group were powerful ladies and successful businesswomen and entrepreneurs.

Over the years many of the members talked with me and showed considerable interest in my views and business experiences, and only because of those who made this effort did I involve myself and become a strong member. In fact, I became the senior (longest sitting) member of the council. Feeling valued, I contributed. Otherwise, I would have just sat there, listened, and left after my first term.

Often, groups do not know how to value others; or they place value on the wrong clues. Let me give an example. A friend of mine was complaining that a particular person he worked with seldom looked him in the eye when speaking. I asked him if he had ever asked the reason. He replied, "No." Having spent considerable time in the culture in which his colleague had been raised, I tried to explain that often it was considered impolite, impertinent, in fact, for a young person to stare an adult in the eye when speaking.

Although you can say the right words, consistent actions and the willingness to learn about people show you value them. Take time to ask people about things you do not understand. Listen, watch, ask, and pay attention before you act. This suggests you care. They, in turn, because they trust your motive, will give you influence in their lives.

TWO:
Separate behavior from worth.
ತಾಂ

A leader must believe people deserve respect regardless of their mistakes, behaviors, or competencies. I know there are evil people, but they are few; and a leader has to work from a different assumption. If you want to lead, you have to separate people's behaviors from their worth. To do otherwise is to disrespect them as human beings. Deal with people's faults and mistakes, but always show respect. Otherwise, they won't trust your motive.

By no means am I a perfect driver. In fact, some would call me a "third-world driver." Now, don't become upset with me; I am a safe and courteous driver. On one occasion I turned right illegally and was pulled over by a police officer, who was not particularly polite. He kept on his sunglasses, offered no explanation, and in curt terms asked me for my license, my registration, and my proof of insurance. There was no "please" or "thank you." His manner, of course, made me suspect his motive.

He sauntered back to his patrol car and was gone a long time. Eventually, he returned to my window, stuffed the ticket inside, and said only that I needed to pay by such and such date or appear in court on another date. Without further comment, he walked away.

I sat there for a while because I was angry. Then I called a colleague of mine who worked for the police department and asked if I could have a jury trial for a traffic ticket. He laughed at me and said, "Lloyd, just pay the fine."

Why was I angry? The officer mixed my behavior with my worth. I felt like a criminal. He was not at all polite, and he did not show interest in teaching me anything or explaining anything to me. If he had said, "Mr. Lewan, I pulled you over because you made an illegal and unsafe right turn where it is expressly forbidden by sign" and suggested that he appreciated my courtesy as he handed me my ticket, I would have paid the fine and not had a second thought. It was my fault, after all.

Most police are great! But, with police work it is so easy to lose this point: Leaders must separate behavior from worth. Police are constantly faced with extreme behavior, usually illegal and criminal. When confronted with resistance, car chases, and such, tempers may flare or patience may grow short, which can result in the use of too much force.

My point is not about police work. It is that leaders — whether they lead agencies, families, corporations, universities, or governments — must be able to separate behavior from worth in all their actions. Otherwise, the leaders' motives are suspect.

I chaired the board of directors for a large human-services organization in Denver. One of the programs served pregnant teens and their babies. They are nice kids. They are not bad; they only made choices that carried difficult consequences. Those who work with these young people have to believe this, or their effectiveness to help is reduced.

As a young United States Marine Corps officer, I was once in charge of a number of special units on my base. One of these was a correctional custody and motivational unit for those marine recruits who were not motivated to succeed. I bumped heads with the mental-health professionals, not over diagnosis, but over the fact that labels were being used widely by the drill instructors in charge and even among the recruits themselves in this motivational unit.

The three categories identified were PA, PD, and PI. They stood for passive aggressive, passive dependent, and pseudo inadequate – the last one alluding to "not too sharp mentally." In any event, I have no quarrel with the field of psychology or the value of accurate diagnosis – if used properly, privately, and in confidence. But, for a recruit to hear every day that he was a PA, PD, or PI from his marine drill instructors was a violation of this principle of the separation of behavior from worth. The privates in the motivational platoon should have been called Private Green, Private Smith, Private Jones, not PA, PD, or PI.

Near the end of a Semester at Sea voyage, a group of faculty and staff discussed ways to improve the program. Many of the suggestions were excellent. This one, however, disturbed me: "If we could get rid of those bad students from party schools, we would be better off." I knew what they meant. Yes, some students do not study; some students are not motivated; some students do not seem to care about schoolwork; and some students occasionally exhibit disruptive behavior. But, what is a bad student?

Asked to evaluate a group of individuals for potential leadership qualities in a corporation, I listened to their chatter over lunch. I heard "the jerk," "that fool," and "he's lame." Derogatory terms about a person violate the concept of separation of behavior from worth. Remember, everything said or done suggests motive.

A leader may fire an employee who fails to do what is expected, may lock up a person who has committed a crime, may fail a student who does not do the work in the classroom, may discipline an individual who is out of control; but a leader may never call a person a "fool," a "jerk," an "idiot," or any other term that diminishes that person and shows a lack of respect.

This commandment is not offered to excuse people from poor behavior. It is offered because leaders deal with tough and difficult situations, and they must separate behavior from worth in the process. If not, they forfeit the chance to have a long-term, positive relationship and impact on their followers. This is a tough stand, but it is essential.

We are inundated with labels in this country: educable, trainable, democrat, republican, conservative, liberal. Just read the papers. I realize that labels help in explanation; but they are dangerous, especially for leaders, because labels mix behavior with worth. Take, for example, the following headlines that might appear in a newspaper:

> *Black gang member shoots three*

> *Gang member shoots three*

Which is more suitable for a leader to use? While there appears to be little difference, there is, in fact, a huge difference.

I love the way congressmen and women address each other on the floor of the house: the gentleman or the gentlewoman from Idaho, not the Italian-Catholic gentleman or gentlewoman from New York. Yes, this is only semantics. But, the latter is more descriptive; and some labels, such as Black or Italian-Catholic, set off prejudice. This may be acceptable for journalists, but leaders must watch how they phrase their thoughts because followers are watching and trying to determine the motive for what their leaders do.

Respect for "other ways" is also at the heart of this demand. When we begin a voyage around the world on our ship, I ask students to take this silent pledge: "Regardless of what behaviors I experience from the people in the ports of call we are about to visit, I will ask myself, first, what needs are these people attempting to meet that are identical to my own."

My years of travel have taught me that we all have the same needs — food, shelter, safety, places for worship, employment, actualization, happiness, appreciation, and love. Boiled octopus, blood with cow's milk, pig fat, grasshoppers, or, in my case, peanut butter and jelly all represent foods of choice to satisfy hunger. St. Peter's in Rome, the Wailing Wall in Israel, the Blue Mosque in Turkey, and the reclining Buddha in Malaysia all represent our need for a spiritual aspect in life.

Differences in the ways we choose to meet our common needs are called culture. With all their peculiarities, different cultures are simply different ways to meet needs; and if we don't understand this, we will never fully appreciate other cultures and/or differences.

If you want to lead, you must separate behavior (culture, ways, choices) from each individual's right to be treated with dignity in everything. Dignity would be nice in all human interaction, although not likely; but it is a must in a leader's actions.

Leaders seldom make decisions with which all agree, but they must treat all people respectfully. This will go a long way in bringing harmony between honest differences. Listen to people speaking on television on the numerous evening public-interest programs. While disagreement is natural, you would think some should be tarred and feathered for what they have done if you listen to the one speaking. Is there no respect for honest differences, or is this just "show biz"?

THREE:
Speak in your own voice.

ॐॐ

Give direction in your own name if you want people to follow you. They will trust your motive more.

So many people today pass the buck. "The VP says." "The university insists." "The policy reads." "The powers-to-be want." That is the easy way. This commandment of influence does not mean that you should not follow the directives of your organization; but, if you want to lead, you must speak in your own voice, showing you accept responsibility for the decisions of the organization for which you work. Equally important, you show you have the courage to be a part of the organization in good faith. This brings more respect and more followership.

Occasionally, a student violates the signed agreement outlining the standards of conduct for Semester at Sea. As the senior official on board for Semester at Sea when I sail, it is my duty to dismiss that student from the program when his/her behavior is particularly egregious, repetitive, or disruptive to the shipboard community. I never say, "I have no choice but to send you home." Rather, I talk with the student, stating the reason and accepting responsibility for the dismissal: "I am sending you home because you violated your agreement with us." In large part, the decision to dismiss a student is a decision in the hands of the dean after much counsel, investigation, and listening. Speak in your own voice. You will be trusted more.

While a young Marine Corps officer, I learned this lesson the hard way. A very senior officer in my chain-of-command (okay, the general) asked me as officer of the day to go to the mess hall and to tell the gunnery sergeant in charge that the corn-on-the-cob was consistently overcooked. The general was a gourmet and wanted it boiled for ten minutes, not a second more.

I grumbled to myself, irritated over the fact that as a Marine Corps officer I was now in charge of the corn. Reluctantly, I drove to the eating area, found the sergeant in charge, and said, "The general has a hair somewhere that is bothering him. To keep him happy, please boil the corn-on-the-cob, at least today, for only ten minutes."

What I did not realize was that the general had come to this mess hall, as well, to have his lunch. When I turned away from the sergeant, I was facing the general; and he had overheard me. He looked me right in the eye and said, "Captain, I don't need you if that's the best you can do."

Was he right? Absolutely. I did not have the courage, *the leadership*, to speak in my own voice as the officer of the day: "Sergeant, would you please boil the corn-on-the-cob for ten minutes." Period.

People will follow you and will trust you as their leader if you do not blame uncomfortable decisions you have to make on others or on circumstances. Give direction in your own name. It engenders more respect and speaks to your motive.

FOUR:
Seek an improved batting average, not perfection or comparison with others.

༺✦༻

This sounds simple, but it is tough. You must always seek to improve the performances, the batting averages, if you will, of those you lead. That is what your followers expect and appreciate. Again, it helps them trust your motive toward them if they believe that is what you are doing.

The best baseball players seldom hit over .350 – that is 350 hits out of a 1000 times at bat. Now, if that is the best for ball players, why do we expect so much from followers?

The secret of leadership is to assign a realistic entering batting average to a new player or employee, based upon his/her education and training and your sense of things. Then your obligation is to help your player improve this average. That is what leadership is about, freeing talent. Remember? If you set an entering expectation that is too high or too low, you will have difficulty helping a follower. Spend more time setting a reasonable expectation. It will make it much easier to help improve the player's performance later.

FIVE:
Spend as much time on the *how* and on the *when* as on the *what.*

೧⁊ৎ

Most meetings I have attended over the years are spent on *what* to do with various kinds of situations – finances, personnel, operations. Yet, over these same years, I have discovered that *how* you explain and present your decisions, *how* you involve people in these results, and *when* you do it show more *respect* for those who are affected by *what* you do.

Even though I may regret telling the following story, here goes: A number of students on a Semester at Sea voyage decided to swim nude after our final port of call (only the Atlantic crossing was left before we were to reach home). Now, please understand that this has happened to me only once in thirty plus years and that our students are serious, great kids, and usually respectful. But, once in awhile they go for it! The group was large enough to be noticed by all on board. Hence, the nude swimming was reported to me in a dozen ways and, of course, with enthusiasm and/or disgust depending on how the person bringing the incident to my attention viewed this behavior.

After contemplating the situation from afar, I said to myself, "Lloyd, you are the leader. What you do is important, but the how and the when are equally important."

With this in mind, I went to my cabin, picked up a little help, and headed for the pool. When I was safely above the pool, perhaps thirty feet, I simply watched for ten minutes. I knew if I was anywhere near the students that I would soon be nude, and this would not be by choice. After awhile I pulled out my helper. With my cheap camera, no film, but a lot of extra flashcubes, I started flashing. You never saw so many bare butts in your life scampering up those ladders. I knew they did not want their bare rear ends on my film, and I also knew they had had their fun.

The mission was accomplished. Students were out of the pool – the *what*. The method did not insult or disrespect the participants; in fact, it appealed to their sense of humor – the *how*. Finally, I took my time before camera flashing – the *when*.

This may seem to be a silly example, but it does come right to the point; and one can easily extrapolate this into any organizational situation.

Another incident happened in Spain. Again, we were at the last port. Looking forward to the final leg of our voyage (a long leg I might add), quite a few students were still on the pier celebrating at a local pub. Our security officer came to me and reported, "I don't think we can sail on time if you want 'that bunch' on board."

Once again, I thought to myself, "It is not the what, but the how and the when." In order to sail, I needed those students on board ship. Taking a plastic trash bag from one of the trash cans on the ship, I walked slowly to where the students were in this mostly outside pub. A few broken bottles littered the ground. Without looking a student in the eye, I got down on my hands and knees and started picking up broken glass. If I smiled or looked at any of those students, of whom I had grown very fond, I would have had a beer in my hand; and I don't even drink. I knew they would not disrespect me because I had served them all these months the best I could. Within a few minutes, they were all headed for the gangway, looking back at me on my hands and knees.

Some years ago I asked a college intern who was working with our company to draft a written policy that would broaden the work schedule so our employees could have more flexibility in their workday, perhaps 6 a.m. through 6 p.m. I gave her three conditions: the employees must be safe, a responsible person must be around, and the customers and the company must be served well. This was the *what*.

You should have read draft number one! In short (and it was not short, it was four pages), it read in part – the *how* – "after a snow day and in relation to all other holidays…" and so forth and so forth that it lost the point. It was so defensive and with so many provisions that it no longer seemed like a benefit.

A great deal can be taught in a story. This is about the *how*. The business writer, Tom Peters observed: "The best leaders…almost without exception and at every level, are master users of stories and symbols."

On each of my voyages with Semester at Sea, I always host a story hour. It is fun and well attended. The students in their pajamas and with their sleeping bags stay with me for hours. To an observer it might seem like entertainment; but, to me, it is more of a teaching time as a moral underlies each story, stories that total to a thirty-plus-year history of a great concept, shipboard education. I don't want to be an entertainer. I want to be a leader, and stories are helpful.

As leaders we make difficult decisions. That is the *what* we do, but we need to work as hard on the *how* and the *when*. This speaks volumes about our motives toward those who follow.

SIX:
Demonstrate grace under pressure.

❧❦

Leadership is tough. Franz Kafka wrote, "In a fight between you and the world, bet on the world."

Leadership, my experience has taught me, is almost antithetical to human nature. All that is being asked of you in this book and the other works on leadership is for you to be super human most of the time. Unfortunately, your human nature often diverts you to isolation, self-pity, anger, disgust, and so forth. You must resist the pressure of your human nature. The only additional advice I can give to help you handle pressure is that the best guarantee of tomorrow is the best today. Give your all each and every day.

As I leave my office each day, I symbolically put a badge on my chest that reads "badge of honor." I was able to absorb my share of the troubles, the "heat," the pressures of my organization's daily endeavors and activities.

If a leader can take up the slack, it frees the rest to do a better job with a greater degree of satisfaction. A leader is like a battery, having positive and negative poles; and one of the functions of a leader is to take the heat and to handle it. The late President Truman said, "If you can't stand the heat, stay out of the kitchen." This is so true.

Even more important than being able to take the heat is the relief it gives those being served. If the leader is "blamed" for a tough decision, then the others can more easily get on with the job.

If I am to show you my motive as your leader, then I must be able to show you I am willing to take it for you and from you. I know this does not sound fair; but, remember, *leadership is about service. It is a one-way street.*

Only under pressure do we find the true character of a leader. It is easy to teach school on the first day of class, but try the week before the mid-year holiday break. That is when students see which teachers can lead. When a football team is winning a game by twenty-one points, it is easy to be a humble and even-tempered coach. In contrast, be a coach in the locker room after a tough loss; that is when real leadership is tested.

Perhaps you work for a corporation. Your voice mail is full. Your to-do list could choke a horse. Your boss wants two projects today, and one of your associates needs some time with you as he is confused about the project you asked him to do. See if you can lead others under these pressures. That is when you find out if you are truly a leader!

Before sailing on a voyage with Semester at Sea, the executive dean is involved in the hiring process; and, of course, one of the explanations each applicant is given about shipboard life is that it involves living in close quarters. Work and personal life are in the same space. Staff and faculty grow tired and lose their way under the daily pressures. It is like being in the middle of an escalator with no escape. They do not have a weekend to themselves for months. When candidates are asked how they handle pressure, the answer is always the same: "I handle pressure well." But, this is not always the case. Over the years I have seen many, who when reaching a certain point in the voyage, struggle because of these unusual pressures.

For a professional, are these pressures any less? Of course not. If you want to lead, you must pace yourself, remain consistent, and handle stress without notice. It is very important to demonstrate that you can give more, can take more, and can still remain the leader. Many people will argue that this is impossible and even ridiculous. I remain convinced that demonstrating grace under pressure is a necessary requirement for a leader. In the final analysis, as the proof of the pudding is in the taste, the proof of leadership is in the pressure.

SEVEN:
Fire people or help people.

಄೦

Hoping that certain employees will quit or fail, managers and supervisors will leave them to flounder. This tactic is not acceptable in leadership. Leaders must ensure that all whom they serve receive the help needed to do the job asked of them. Think about those being served. Are they being helped and encouraged? If not, why not?

When a leader, a manager, or a supervisor comes to me to complain or to tell me of an employee's weakness or failure, my first two questions are

- What have you done to help him/her?
- What are his/her strengths?

Yes, the worker's weakness may be real or the behavior may be wrong, but s/he is entitled to receive help. If not, then fire him/her. To leave the employee alone or to build a case against him/her is not kind, and it does not demonstrate leadership.

Be more creative in helping. Send notes, ask questions, spend a little time. One of the best ways to help is using second-party compliments. Tell one who will tell another that you appreciate an employee's efforts, work, accomplishments, and, as appropriate, attitude.

Your motive toward those who follow you determines the influence they will give you, and knowing that you will try to help them encourages them to trust your motive.

EIGHT:
Listen to people.

అతని

Motive and listening go hand in hand. Audrey Brodt, PhD. wrote, "Understanding is more productive than advice." It is painfully obvious that most people in the work environment do not feel that anyone listens enough.

No other behavior on the part of a leader is more attractive than listening. You can talk well, look people in the eye, pat them on the shoulder, or send them notes; however, when you just sit and listen to them when they feel like talking says so much more about your *motive*. Time is precious; but, if you want to lead, you must take time to listen.

NINE:
Keep your eye on the faithful.
ॐ∼

Followers must believe that leaders will keep their eyes on them when they have been faithful. *They count on their leaders to "stand tall" in their name when they do the job as agreed.*

Please read the following very carefully, for it is very important to leadership:

Particulary in American culture, a single act, a one-time success, a moment in the sun becomes to a large measure what people are thought to be. America is very much a culture of snips, clips, and sound bites – one great game of football, a power-house speech aired on television, one act of kindness, one book milked into many. It is not that the aforementioned acts are not good or important. Rather, it is that they do not always represent the faithful ones, those who get the job done year in and year out.

Faithful followers want to know that their leaders will see through hype, self-promotion, and one-time spotlight stuff. If their leaders do not see this, who will? Moreover, if leaders do not look for the faithful, the world will be filled with "chest beaters," people saying, "Did you see *my* proposal? *I* did that. That was *my* idea." This is tough. Yet, if followers are going to trust their leaders' motives, they must know leadership will see through hype and will notice faithfulness.

Following are a plethora of examples for that is how important this principle is:

◆ The United States Marine Corps motto reads, *Sempre Fideles* (Always Faithful). I had dinner recently with Hugh O'Brien, Wyatt Earp of television fame. He has a national program for high-school leaders, and we are looking for ways to cooperate with one another. I trust his commitment partly because of our common Marine Corps heritage. Similarly, Tom Johnson, the CEO of the corporation to which we sold our company, was the leader we sought. He also was a marine. In our initial discussions, I trusted his word because we, too, shared this common Marine Corps bond.

◆ While I am very reluctant to tell the following story, it so makes the point. For seventeen years, I have played Santa Claus on Christmas Day at The Children's Hospital in Denver. The volunteer staff at this hospital knows that I want to remain anonymous, for often a media group asks to follow Santa. This day means a lot to me. I receive far more than I give, for those who are confined to their beds on holidays are really sick and show extraordinary courage. I wake up early, drive to the hospital, put on my red suit (and my other "stuff"), work with the head nurse in providing a few gifts, and then go room to room. I play, talk, hug – whatever feels right.

My point: This is okay, and I am glad to do it; but it is insignificant in comparison to the many other volunteers who give so much at The Children's Hospital year in and year out. Emily Selig lives next door to me. She is well over eighty years old (sorry, Emily), and she is one of these other volunteers. She holds very sick babies and helps in many different ways on so many days. Her volunteer badge shows how many hours she gives. *She is the faithful one* and the one whom the media should follow.

◆ During one of my earlier voyages, the academic dean and I told the faculty and the staff that we would be pleased to write out a few comments about their performances if they would like. In the last days of the semester, one faculty member asked me to do this. I wrote something about his acceptance by the students and his teaching abilities. I told him I thought he had done a "satisfactory" job.

After he read it, he asked to see me for one hour. Of course, I granted his request. In short, he said to me, "At the beginning of the voyage, you said that faculty would be judged on three items: their teaching abilities, their understanding of their particular subject and area of the world, and how they helped students juxtapose the classroom into the ports of call. Do you know how many years I have spent in Asia? Do you know how many hours I have spent with students in the union talking about Chinese, Japanese, and Malaysian art and architecture? Do you know how many students I traveled with in port to help them see the art and the art objects in Asia?"

I said, "No," to all of his questions. He told me that he was disappointed. He made his point. But, more importantly, I changed my evaluation to "above average." I had not seen his faithfulness in what was asked of him. My evaluation was neither complete nor fair.

This experience taught me a number of lessons. One, you have to ask people, in evaluation, to share what they have done. You will probably learn much you did not know. Two, I was not practicing responsible leadership, for I was not honoring the faithful.

◆ I enjoy football; and one of my good friends is Randy Gradishar, a past football great. He was an Ohio State draft pick and linebacker with the Denver Broncos for ten years in the '70's and the '80's. What impressed me most about Randy, besides his athletic ability, was his faithfulness; he played every game during those years and always displayed a great attitude. He was one of the faithful ones. (For those who love football, you will remember him as a member of the great 1977 Denver Broncos Orange Crush defense.)

◆ Our best sales people are those who, without boasting, year in and year out, good times and bad, make our President's Club as top producers. Fortunately, we have many men and women who meet these criteria. One good month is not enough. One good year is good, but year in and year out is faithful.

Beryle Markham in *West with the Night* said, "If a man has any greatness in him, it comes to light not in one flamboyant hour but in the ledger of his daily work."

Leaders should be the ones who notice, who appreciate, and who see to it that faithfulness is recognized. In a statistics class, I learned that validity and reliability are two tests of a survey instrument. Reliability refers to the test's ability to test the same thing *repeatedly*. This must be true of leaders. They must see the faithful ones doing their job over and over.

TEN:
Help people gain perspective and context for their work, mission, lives, and messes.

☙❧

The three behaviors of influence that I find myself practicing most often are valuing those I serve, separating behavior from worth, and this tenth commandment. If you take the time to give people a context, a perspective, about their issues, they can then go back and do it better for themselves. What more could be asked of you as a leader? People will trust your motive if you can do this for them.

Most of us live in a fairly narrow world. We see the world from our own experiences. It is like being in a theater, seeing the stage and the play from only one seat. We might see something else if we could watch the same play from many seats. This is what leaders can do for others. Because leaders tend to have more experience and a wider view of the world to share, one of their tasks is to help people see better so people may do better.

Arthur C. Clarke, the distinguished author I mentioned earlier, sailed on several Semester at Sea voyages with me. On one of these voyages, I asked him to respond to a lecture about population that was given one morning in our core class. When the lecturer finished, Clarke stood and said that he had nothing to say if that was the lecturer's view of the world. The lecturer had used a world map with America in the center and Asia split in half. We use this map a lot in the United States. Perspective and context.

When I was young, the dominant magazine in our home was *LIFE*. Then *People* came along, then *Us*, and now I see *SELF* on the grocery store shelves. I am waiting for a magazine called *Me*, although I did see a journal entitled *All About Me* in a bookstore. We have become a little narcissistic in this country, a bit self-focused and self-absorbed.

To focus only on one's personal world is understandable for people in general, but this is unacceptable for a leader. To lead, a person must have a wider view.

Lewan & Associates, Inc. was listed in *Inc.* magazine in 1982 as one of the 500 fastest growing companies in America. We were proud, but in context don't get too impressed.

It is much easier when a company is relatively new to grow at rates whose percentage growth looks good. For example, $3,000 to $6,000 is a 100% growth. In reality, the real success stories are those companies who are still in business and who are still profitable twenty years later.

Context is important with all claims of greatness. Lists are helpful, but they are also deceiving if not carefully defined.

In a statistics course I took as an under-graduate, I read the book *How to Lie with Statistics* by Darrell Huff. One section pointed out that even statistics have a perspective. An undefined statistic is of no value or context. On a cereal box, for example, I saw the following chart. Displaying undefined values, the chart communicated nothing.

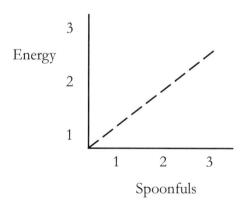

Perspective and context come with personal experience and by learning from others who have seen more. On a Semester at Sea voyage, a group of students and I visited the Taj Mahal, that great marble monument in Agra, India, built for the love of a woman. While in the air on an Indian Airline flight, a young student next to me remarked, "Thank God, I am an American." Everything was getting to him – the poverty, the food, the number of people he had seen, and the lack of cleanliness. This was his first day in the country, a country of great contrasts – rich and poor, beautiful and ugly, successful and struggling.

As an educator, I would have gladly stood on my soapbox and preached on Indian culture, open-mindedness, tolerance, diversity, and the purposes of international study among other great subjects; but I knew at that moment this would have gone right over his head. He did not want to hear anything. He was experiencing India for the first time.

Moreover, my preaching would have only made matters worse for him because I have always secretly wanted to be appointed United States Ambassador to India. If there was ever a land that spoke volumes to the two ends of humanity, it is

India. India is everything a person can experience, all in one great nation of two billion people.

I kept my mouth shut, enjoyed our visit to the Taj Mahal, and returned to our ship with the group. Two days later, without comment, I put a piece of paper, a portion of an article reprinted and often used by social scientists, on his cabin door.

> Dawn finds our patriot garbed in pajamas, a garment of East Indian origin, lying in a bed built on a pattern originated in either Persia or Asia Minor. He looks out a window made of glass invented by ancient Egyptians and washes with soap invented by the Gauls. As he has breakfast, his fork is a medieval Italian invention and his spoon a copy of a Roman original. His food and drink are placed before him in pottery vessels. The popular name of which, china, is sufficient evidence of their origin. He will probably sweeten his coffee with sugar, discovered in India. Before going out, and if it looks like rain, he puts on outer shoes of rubber discovered by the ancient Mexicans and takes an umbrella invented in India. On his way to the train, he pauses for a moment to buy a newspaper, paying for it with coins invented in ancient Lydia. Once on the train, he settles in for a

cigar invented in Brazil and reads the news of the day, imprinted in characters invented by the ancient Semites by a process invented in Germany upon a material invented in China. As he scans foreign trouble, he will thank a Hebrew God in an Indo-European language that he is one hundred percent American!

Written by Ralph Linton and published in *The American Mercury* magazine in 1937, this article is entitled "One Hundred Percent American." This is perspective! America is great, but all things and ideas did not come from America. Some even came from India!

I perform better as a leader when I understand more, see a wider view, or experience the lot of another.

Working with urban issues, particularly related to gang activity, I have always felt perspective and context are such underutilized strategies. People who have experienced another part of the world are permanently and positively affected. To take several hundred gang leaders from Los Angeles to Calcutta, India, would give them an entirely different view of their homes, their schools, and their personal lives in America. What an idea. Perspective.

Most alienation, I have learned, is a matter of limited perspective and context as much as anything else. How about a disgruntled employee going to another corporation for a month? Perhaps this worker's view of his/her own company would change.

At times we ask salespeople to ride with technicians to see how important our technicians are and vice versa. Sales people do not always appreciate the value of technical service, and technicians do not know how tough it is to cold call for potential customers or to be treated like "dirt" by a receptionist.

You get my point. As leaders one of the great ways of showing perspective and context is giving your associates a small opportunity to experience a wider view.

Perspective is a part of leadership however you chose to introduce it. On the Semester at Sea Fall 2000 sail, my associate dean and his wife brought their two-year-old twins with them. Watching them manage these toddlers during the voyage, college students kiddingly said that this was the best birth control on the ship. Perspective!

Leaders must provide perspective and context so those who follow can see better and, thereby, do better. At a social gathering I attended, many in the group were complaining under the general theme: America has so many problems. It bothered me greatly. I reminded them of an Associated Press report in that day's paper explaining that, fearing slaughter, one million Hutus fled to Zaire. This was after thousands were already slaughtered. Perspective.

I overheard our company president the other day defending our CEO, who also is our financial guru. Our president said to a sales group, "What do you think would happen to the company if we always did want we wanted to do?" After the laughter died and some serious thought was applied, the answer was, "We would be out of business." Perspective and context. They are the key. Leaders, please think about it.

I cannot leave this idea of perspective and context without one strategy that has always served me well in helping others see and understand more. Most everything can be framed on a continuum so both sides or the two extremes are seen. Great teachers use this method. This is not being relativistic or without values; it is just looking at the bigger picture before you act as a leader. Of course, you may believe anything you wish from your view or perspective, even an absolute value; yet, remember, those you serve do not always hold the same view. If you want to lead, you must attempt to broaden your view so more are included. Let me explain myself.

As stated, one of the main purposes of this book is to introduce leadership as separate from management. Let's see this as a governing continuum.

```
┌─────────────────────────────────────────┐
│                                         │
│              GOVERNANCE                 │
│   Management _____ Leadership   │
│                                         │
└─────────────────────────────────────────┘
```

Most, I think, would agree that leadership and management are different. Again, this is the easy part. The tough part is defining how they are different. This is where a continuum helps. Neither end is good or bad. They are simply the outer edges of organizational governance. Both are important. Both are needed. But, there is a difference.

The continuum helps you understand where you are and where your organization is within these two concepts once they are defined for you. Maybe you and your organization are satisfied with where you are. This is all well and good; but, if you need improvement, a continuum helps you think about it. Do you want or need more management? Do you want or need more leadership?

In my book *Women in the Workplace: A Man's Perspective*, the continuum addressed therein was this:

GENDER

Men _____Women

See Objects   See Relationships Between Objects

Most of us would agree there is a difference between men and women, but that's the easy part. The tough part, again, is determining *how* they are different, in general or in terms worth thinking about. That is the question I attempted to tackle in the book.

Let me give a final example. If you wanted to view the Clinton presidency with a group who held many different views, this would be a difficult task, to say the least. Yet, if you offered five continua or ways to discuss President Clinton's terms in office, you might stand a chance of guiding or focusing the discussion and, more importantly, of finding a little common ground for an altered view or at least a wider understanding.

CLINTON'S PRESIDENCY
discussed as…

Republican _____ Democrat
Conservative _____ Liberal
Immoral _____ Moral
Public Life _____ Private Life
His Behavior _____ His Worth

As leaders we try to find the smallest point of agreement as a beginning for our responsibility of reconciliation, and the way we frame issues helps make this possible. For example, at the conclusion of the Korean War, while it took days to even agree on the kind of table and how the participants in the peace negotiations were to be seated, this was at least a start.

We all have varying views, beliefs, and experiences; and it is the leader who has to try to bridge these into some common agreement or understanding. It is a tough job. Chances are better, however, if those who follow trust the leader's motive.

As a leader you make decisions, inspire, focus, and follow through on what is important; but you must treat people right, as well, so they may catch a glimpse of your motive. One of the best ways to treat people right is to help them see better – perspective.

స్త్రీర్ఖ్య

A very special woman, one of the best, served with me on one of the voyages of Semester at Sea I was privileged to lead. A particular student had given us a great deal of difficulty (maybe I should say grief); and she finally announced to me, "I want you to see him." Seeing the anger in her face, I asked her what was her motive for me to see the student. She responded, "Punish him good."

She was the best director of student life one could have; but the senior leader, me in this case, must always try to teach before giving way to punishment. I saw the student as she requested, but only after we agreed that teaching him something was our mutual motive and would govern my interaction with him and only after she cooled off. She kids me about this to this day, but we both agree that *motive is everything in leadership.*

Chapter Nine

PERSONAL vs. POSITION POWER

Personal vs. Position Power

The point of this chapter is simple: *Leaders must know who they are.* For me this has been a recognition of two power sources – *personal power* and *position power*. To balance and to understand the two is essential, and a two-to-one ratio of personal to position power is minimum to ensure the humility required when given any kind of leadership authority.

Personal Power

Personal power has two parts. First is *being peaceful.* We use self-esteem a lot in our literature and discussion, but I prefer peaceful. None of us has absolute self-esteem, but all of us can become peaceful.

Looking at a few of the great disciplines in the academic world, we see that the reconciliation of several parts makes it whole – Yin and Yang in philosophy; super ego, ego, and id in psychology; spiritual and human nature in religion; rational and non rational in sociology; and left and right brain in medicine. Most gain wholeness from reconciliation. For me it is especially the reconciliation of my human and spiritual nature. I am at peace with myself, for I know that I have God's hand on me.

To see how peaceful I am each day, I notice how I drive. If I am erratic, rushed, or a little irritated, I know I am not peaceful.

Some years ago, when I was driving to the local Jenny Craig center, I accidentally cut off a guy driving a truck. He gave me a gesture with his finger. Reading his lips and noticing the gun rack in his back window, I decided to drive quickly to the local police station nearby. When I pulled in, he passed by, gave me another gesture, and revved his engine. I said to myself, "He is not peaceful."

One of the saddest days in my years with our company occurred when one of our technicians was returning to one of our branch offices. While driving on an interstate, he found himself in a male road-rage situation. The other driver, with his wife and child in the car, followed him off the interstate into a grassy area and shot him several times with a pistol. Our employee died. This was a sad case of no peace in a life resulting in a tragedy.

After giving a keynote address, I love a standing ovation, of course, and am even thrilled with enthusiastic clapping. Yet, in all honesty, if they boo me, I am all right. I told the truth as I saw it, and I did the very best I could. That is what being peaceful is about for me.

You cannot change the world, all the hurts, angers, disquiets, disappointments. But, if you want to be a leader, you must be peaceful. Look inside yourself and find some sort of peace your own way.

The second part of personal power is *knowing the difference between working colleagues and a human-survival unit*. Some would call this family. If you study any culture on earth, at the heart is a human-survival unit – a few individuals and small communities of individuals with whom you have trust, have full reciprocity, share values, and enjoy unconditional love. You can count on them!

Without these few precious individuals and groups, people do not come to work healthy. They may need more from their colleagues than can be expected and may focus more on their personal needs while at work than on the objectives of employment. Most people who work cannot live up to this difficult demand, but a leader must. A leader must have a human-survival unit in place before offering to lead.

Women taught me the difference between colleagues and human-survival units. With their heightened interest in the value of relationships, many women, I believe, enjoy and have a more acute understanding about human-survival units – family, friends, neighbors, and places of worship.

Let me tell you about a few of those who constitute my human-survival unit. First are my brother, Paul; his wife, Marjorie; and their three children. I am grateful for the bond Paul and I have had all these years and for the ways that Marjorie has always encouraged me to be close to their children. Seventeen years ago, two young boys without a dad in their lives hooked up with me when they were twelve and eight, respectively. We have no legal connection, but we did agree to be in each other's lives for as long as we live. I care a lot for these two. They probably would not say I am anything great, but I know they would say they can count on me. I also have a few special friends without whom my life would be so much less. They know who they are and why they are so important to me.

One evening my nephew, Matt, a young teen at the time, was burned quite severely when he and a friend were kicking around a lighted tennis ball soaked in gasoline. The tennis ball hit Matt in the chest, spewed gasoline, and set him on fire. During one of my shifts with him in the hospital's burn unit, he said to me, "If something ever happens to my dad, do you become my father?" I responded, "No, Matt. No one can replace your dad, but you can count on me to the end of my life." This is a human-survival unit!

A friend in my survival unit was very badly burned, along with her infant son, in a propane explosion. What a tragedy. I am privileged to chair the board of directors for her small, not-for-profit organization dedicated to preventing burns and assisting children who have been burned. She is a special friend. My point is that if it were not for her human-survival unit during her recovery – her son, her mom and dad, her brother, and her grandmother – she has told me many times that she would have given up. The pain and the fear of what she would look like were just too great to bear. She especially wanted to survive for the most important member of her survival unit, her son. She found the courage.

That's all you get, a few special people in your life who make up your human-survival unit. Know who they are, for they have so much to do with your ability to come to work healthy. Even more important, know the difference between these few and your many working colleagues and acquaintances. It really has an impact on great leadership.

As mentioned earlier, I have worked with a not-for-profit organization dedicated to keeping young children away from gang activity and membership. When I think of a human-survival unit, I quickly go to the "gang" idea. The gang purports to be a friend, to make young people feel like they belong, to let them participate, to suggest they have others they can count on, to make them feel equal. Statistics and interviews show this to be bankrupt; but, with a failed family or the lack of another healthy human-survival unit in a young man's or woman's life, it is easy to see how gangs can be attractive. Thousands across all socio-economic and cultural boundaries belong to gangs in America.

◆ ◆ ◆

In all of the years that I have recommended people for leadership, I looked for *this* personal power. It usually shows itself in men and women who know who they are. They are *grounded in their lives* and are not always looking for something better over the fence. They are usually *low maintenance* and *able to be on their own* without much supervision or external motivation. Additionally, they are *easy to deal with* and *have their heads in their work.*

For years I served on a statewide council of which there were a number of persons with doctoral degrees. Most of the time I was listed as Lloyd Lewan, whereas others were listed as Dr. Smith or J. Brown, PhD. Actually, I *preferred* it. A low profile suits a leader better *because* of personal power.

The leader knows who s/he is, without title. I have been just "Lloyd" to the thousands of students I have sailed with. The right kind of respect comes to those who have personal power. Respect doesn't come in a title.

On the ship a semester or so ago, one of our guests, who had joined the voyage as interport lecturer for the upcoming country of call, confessed while having lunch with me, "I thought you were the academic dean. Then, after watching you do all the 'crap,' including carrying my luggage, I knew you were the administrative dean."

Personal power for leaders is more important than position power because it allows them to do the "crap." Leaders always look inside themselves for solutions and strength. They don't blame others for their problems or their circumstances. This takes personal power.

Position Power

Position power, on the other hand, is that which an organization bestows on a leader – title, office, responsibility. Most of us know what this means. Yet, position power without personal power is very dangerous. Leaders can easily feel that what they do is who they are – position and title – but this is not true. I cannot change all those who take their work position power and use and abuse it to be important, but I can help make sure leaders do not become confused. *Personal power is who a person is. Position power is what a person does. Leaders have both.*

Recently, I was privileged to attend a special gathering of people at the home of the governor of Colorado. As we mingled with each other, I noticed that most people who did not know me often started with, "What do you do?" Then they gave me their business card. (I believe they call that networking.) Nothing is wrong with any of this, but it is often only an exercise in exchanging position power.

Position is fine. I am proud of my degrees, my Semester at Sea involvement, my corporate position, and all the other accomplishments that I have worked hard for and earned. It is fine to wear symbols of position power – super bowl rings or academic regalia. Personally, I enjoy commencements because I can wear my doctoral robe. My only caution is that when you wear these symbols be sure you don't take them too seriously and be sure to look back and to focus on those who are not yet there.

In today's workplace most people's issues are not as related to work (their position) as you would think. Many issues are related to this lack of personal power. From time to time a young leader comes to me with a serious issue. Given my belief that two-thirds of a leader's strength is in personal power and one-third is in the strength the organization affords (position power), I try to determine if the issue is work related or personal. I am willing to help in either case, but before helping it is best to know if the issue is an in-work or out-of-work issue. Then it is clear who is responsible.

With employees it is more difficult to separate in-work from out-of-work issues, and often not much can be done with this. But, a leader *must* see the difference and handle his/her personal issues because they will affect his/her ability to lead. Personal power *is* essential if a person wants to lead.

❧

Final comment: A colleague of mine called and said, "I have to hurry. We are having our leadership meeting this morning." What she really meant is that they were having a meeting of those with position power. There is a difference!

A Summary

PERSONAL POWER		POSITION POWER
Peaceful Means:	*Human- Survival Units Ensure:*	*Work Honors:*
Self-respect	Values	Titles
Humor	Commitment	Responsibility
Spirituality	Family	Status
Creativity	Neighborhoods	Colleagues
Self-Love	Schools	Degrees
Liberating	Local Churches	Competencies
Fully Functioning	Unconditional Love	Professional Success
Initiating Structure	Learning	Financial Stability
	Reciprocity	Work Skills

The differences between personal power and position power
are summarized in the table above.

Chapter Ten

ETHICS AND LEADERSHIP

Ethics and Leadership

All that has been asked of a leader in the preceding pages is not quite enough. There is more. Ethics are essential for leadership.

Although I want to refrain from preaching, ethics are critical. A person cannot live up to the expectations of leadership without ethics, which rest on character – honesty, integrity, trustworthiness, dependability, decency, and so much more. The personal ethics of a leader guarantees a belief, a focus, and a motive that is trustworthy.

Author and at-the-time president of the Camden, Maine-based Institute for Global Ethics,

Rushworth Kidder wrote, "Ethics is obedience to the unenforceable."

James Gavin, a retired five star general, more recently an academic, said in an interview, "You lead them well not because you're so great but because they wouldn't let you down."

Remember, followership is a free-will offering. When students on a Semester at Sea voyage change behavior because they do not want to let me down, I am most proud. This is much more effective than punishment.

Although the audience likes to see tough, do not be seduced into tough to impress the audience. The decent man or woman, as leader, does that which is right, not that which brings praise. As James Crook says, "A man who wants to lead an orchestra must turn his back on the world."

Today, the United States Marine Corps addresses character as a part of leadership. They describe military character, in part, as "the sum total of your personality traits." The marine's list of character traits includes integrity, endurance, courage, selflessness, commitment, strong will, tact, justice, decisiveness, and humility, to list a few. While others call this ethics, I call it internal congruence. It is all the same – your personal traits.

In *The Leadership Challenge*, James Kouzes and Barry Posner argue that credibility is the bottom line for leadership. They cite a survey about leadership conducted by the American Management Association, which noted honesty/integrity being listed 83% of the time as most admired.

Many of us who serve as leaders agree with Charles Swindoll, theologian and author, when he says, "I am convinced that life is ten percent what happens to me and ninety percent how I react to it." A positive attitude is a legitimate expectation of "good character."

While your character is framed in your family and in your early years, make no mistake. Character, however defined, is important to leadership as much as skill. Character and ethics are a part of the same notion and determine the way you deal with others. If you choose to be a leader, you must perform at an extraordinary level of commitment and of service *without ego* in the way, *under pressure,* and, at the same time, always *with grace*. This requires character and ethics.

Without Ego

A leader has an ego, of course. We all do, and nothing is wrong with that. It cannot, however, get in the way. Have you ever had a salesperson present so much ego when you first met that you had no interest in the product? It is the same with leadership. Keep your ego in your pocket. Better yet, keep it in the trunk of your car. A servant never comes to serve with an ego hanging out. Humility and quiet strength wear much better on a leader.

Under Pressure

When life is the busiest and you have the most deadlines, you must still provide leadership – excitement, focus, and respect – if you claim the title "leader." I know how difficult it is when you are angry, upset, and discouraged. Yes, even leaders have tough days. But, if you are out of sorts, emotionally uptight, less than objective, and, more importantly, not gracious, wait until you are better before you act because you may cause irreparable harm to those who follow you. Even better, pass the baton to another leader who is in control; or at least tell your followers you are not up to snuff.

And With Grace

Please give this much thought. Gracious is the way of a leader. People expect consistent, gracious behavior from their leaders. This in no way means a leader is unreal, not entitled to emotions, or restricted from making tough decisions; but, as a leader deals with others, gracious (or respectful) behavior is always best. It lasts longer and encourages better results. When football players screw up, some coaches grab them, push them, and swear at them. While this might be football motivation, it is not leadership because it is not gracious.

꼟

Ethics and character are really about decency; and leadership without ethics, and all that ethics implies, is virtually impossible.

Chapter Eleven

ARISTOTLE TO TODAY

Aristotle to Today

So much has been written about leadership; and when you sort through it all, it reads much the same because leadership is a set of principles that remains the same.

To illustrate the aforementioned comment, let me go back into history and visit one of the great Greek philosophers, Aristotle (384-322 B.C.). He said that a leader must have: "Ethos, the moral character to persuade; pathos, the ability to move people emotionally; and logos, the intellect for sound reasoning." Compared to my model presented in Chapter Nine, ethos and pathos (moral character and enthusiasm) are about personal power; logos (intellect) is about position power.

In more recent history, Harry Truman, the United States' thirty-third president and known for his simple and to-the-point comments, was once heard to say, "In periods where there is no leadership, society stands still." He did not say management; he said leadership.

Not too many years ago, I was invited to give a keynote address for a large corporation. Two of the objectives of my time with them were to define leadership in relation to management and to comment on a major study they had commissioned of their management effectiveness. I am not a great student, but I am at least a student and spent considerable time with the study results. While it contained some useful data, not a single comment about leadership, good or bad, was mentioned. This frustrated me.

I was so thankful to the drafters of their study, for they had the good sense to ask for a few subjective comments from a select group of employees. With increasing interest, I read these subjective comments. One of the very last comments rang the loudest bell in my head. I paraphrase, herein, for I believe it says it all about leadership.

This is a so-so company to work for. They work you at a hectic pace, only a fifteen-minute break twice a day, now that's crazy; and they demand a lot with not much fun. *However, my supervisor is such a great person, and only because of my supervisor do I endure such conditions* (italics added).

Leadership always has, always does, and always will make a difference. It is not the same as management. If you do not agree with me, I beg you, at least, to define it for yourself and your organization.

The purpose of this short chapter is to point out that leadership has been the same throughout history. Those who understood it early on are no different from those who understand it today. Management changes with the culture and with improvements in organizational developments, experiences, efficiencies, and electronics, but not leadership. Like great works of art that speak across the centuries, leadership is today what it was yesterday; and it will be the same tomorrow. Excite followers, be the number one believer, be realistic, keep followers focused, and treat them right. This is leadership.

When I speak, I am often asked to name some great leaders in order to relate the principles to actual persons. Before I do, I first ask my audience whom they consider great leaders.

It does not take long to know a lot about who is in the audience. Republicans list republicans, for example, President Ronald Reagan. Democrats list democrats, for example, the late President Franklin D. Roosevelt or the late President John F. Kennedy. Liberals list liberals. Conservatives list conservatives.

Most people, when asked to mention great leaders, pick those with whom they agree. Yet, if the principles of leadership are properly applied, people should also single out leaders with whom they do not agree because leadership is leadership.

Following are some leaders I would choose to single out. (Keep in mind that leaders are not perfect, but they are leaders nonetheless.)

◆ On several occasions I have been privileged to be with Mikhail Gorbachev. He believed that communism had its value. Yet, he realized it was not a realistic economic system for the 21st Century; and he had the courage to try to change it. Unfortunately, he lost control of the change; and it moved beyond him, faster than he had planned or wanted. He paid a price as he was moved aside and unappreciated by many in the former Soviet Union. Nevertheless, he stayed the course and made a difference. He is a great leader. He was realistic enough to change, was focused on what was important, and treated people with great dignity. History will honor him. I do.

◆ Nelson Mandela, in South Africa, was a giant of a leader and met all the criteria. Here is a man who was in prison for nearly thirty years on political grounds. Yet, he retained his belief in an integrated South Africa, was willing to forgive his captors, and at a very late age was able to come out of prison to lead South Africa from apartheid to a more democratic government. Mandela certainly made a difference and paid the price.

◆ Dan Ritchie is the current chancellor at the University of Denver. With excitement, courage, and intellect, he has transformed this university. He was a Westinghouse CEO and retired. With a one-dollar a year salary and under difficult times for the university, he took over as chancellor. He has created a clear vision, has focused all constituencies on his belief for the university, has ensured financing, and has gained the respect of all who have been involved or who have watched the transformation. Moreover, he is always gracious toward those who are with him.

◆   While you may not agree ideologically with Pope John Paul II, he is clearly a leader. There is no question in my mind that he is the number one Roman Catholic on earth, focused totally to his calling and gracious and respectful to all at all times. When he was in Denver a few years ago, he united, excited, and reconciled a whole state in a few days. I am not Catholic, but I was affected.

≈◦≈

We had a guest faculty member from India on one of our Semester at Sea voyages. He was giving us a briefing as we approached Madras, now Chennai, a port in his home country. A student asked him, "If so many people are hungry in India, why don't they eat the cows?"

Our faculty friend sucked in his stomach, tightened his chest, and without hesitation in his colloquial English replied, "Cows is sacred, and 'dat' is 'dat'" (that is that). Religion is a part-and-parcel of Indian life. Cows are sacred to a Hindu, and that is all there is to it. No discussion.

This is also true with leadership. The principles will always stay the same, and "dat" is "dat."

Chapter Twelve

FINAL THOUGHTS

Final Thoughts

In any written endeavor, the writer usually shares some special thoughts or words of encouragement at the conclusion. As I age in leadership, the following thoughts have become more valid. These I give as my words of encouragement to you.

Leaders Must Lead

☙❧

I cannot say it better. William Shedd wrote, "Ships are safe in the harbor, but that's not what ships are built for." A leader has a purpose and has made a promise. A leader must be in the game.

Do Not Become Discouraged

৵৽

You will be criticized always. This is why you have to be strong as well as self-valuing as a leader. If all else fails, remember what Albert Einstein said: "Great spirits have always encountered violent opposition from mediocre minds." That may be a bit harsh, but many will not understand your mission as a leader. As there is not a good place to put this in the book, I add it here. Do not hang around complainers. They will surely drag you down, and you will seldom pull them up.

The Principles of Leadership Have Equality

৵৽

One of the great principles or assumptions of higher education passed on to America from England is the principle of "the equality of disciplines." All subjects or disciplines – physics, history, literature, mathematics – under the auspices of a university are of equal value to society. This is the same with the principles of leadership. All the principles are of equal importance. You must attempt to live up to them all.

The Greater Your Belief, the Greater Your Leadership

❧

The first chief executive officer under China's rule and a friend, Tung Chee Wa of Hong Kong, offered: "As we in Hong Kong face one of the most severe challenges in our recent history, I *deeply believe* that if we can show the same spirit of strength, courage, solidarity, and concern for our fellow citizens, we will be able to overcome our present difficulties and build a brighter future" (italics added). Belief is a large part of what leadership is about.

You Cannot Lead If Conversion Is Your Goal

❧

Conversion can be the goal if you are a missionary or other religious leader. But, if you want to be a head of state or a CEO in a secular and diverse corporation, you must *let followers be who they are* and still find a way to bring them and their values to a *common goal* with you and the organization.

Leadership Is a Habit

☙❧

Leadership is not a part-time job or an assignment. Once you understand it and see its value, it becomes a part of who you are. In short, a leader wears well for the long haul.

Tolerance and Forgiveness
Are at the Heart of Leadership

☙❧

Someone important to me once told me that I am too tolerant (and that may be). He said, "I do not think you have any values." This hurt me a great deal, but then I realized that *tolerance* is one of the greatest values in a free society and is critical to leadership. I make no apology for my tolerances learned so well from the privilege of seeing so much.

Forgiveness is equally important. Mother Teresa advised, "People are often unreasonable, illogical, and self-centered. Forgive them anyway." From his latest book, Archbishop Desmund Tutu of South Africa writes, "because of forgiveness there is a future."

Know the Way of Love

~∞~

From our Judeo-Christian heritage, we learn that love suffers long, love is not puffed up, love is not selfish, love does not hold grudges, love rejoices in the truth, and love never fails (see I Corinthians 13:4-8). Love results in kindness, and you cannot lead without kindness toward those you serve.

Have Faith in the Human Spirit

~∞~

Do you remember reading *Moby Dick* by Herman Melville? I remember one passage in particular: "Men may seem detestable as joint companies and nations; knaves, fools and murderers there may be. Men may have mean and meager faces; but man, in the ideal, is so noble and sparkling, such a grand and glowing creature, that over any ignominious blemish in him all his fellows should run to throw their costliest robes." Human beings are worthy of leadership.

Live by Your Personal Values, Govern by Those Values You Agree to Carry Out

❧❧

Often, leaders are frustrated because their personal values for behavior are so different from those of others in the organization or from those of the organization itself. No one can be that congruent. Leaders must live their lives strictly by their personal values but must be as tolerant as they can toward others.

The Walk of a Leader Is from Rationality to Wisdom

❧❧

Intelligence is important, knowledge is needed, but experience is the distinguishing mark of a leader because *it leads to wisdom*. Followers deserve nothing less. Many bright people live in our world, but they are not necessarily wise. Consider the many uneducated, hard-working mothers who raise large families and who direct them through much. Their children always seek their counsel and wisdom. Similarly, those who follow you are looking to you for counsel and wisdom.

Leadership Is, at Best, Muddling Through

~~~

Leaders largely reconcile factions – never pretty, at best mudding *through*, *but always getting through*. Honor leadership, for leadership is not easy.

Finally, and most importantly,

A Leader Always Goes Higher for Advice and Counsel

~~~

Eagles do not flock as the well-known saying suggests; hence, it is hard for a leader to find help and perspective for him/herself.

As a leader I need help, too. I find someone who has more experience, who is wiser, and for whom I hold great respect. And, *I can go no higher than to my knees.*

So many variables affect leadership. If you want to practice leadership, however, you must first seek to understand it. Hopefully, this book has helped.

Remember,

- ⫽ Leadership is a skill separate from management.

- ⫽ We must be able to define leadership to have it.

- ⫽ Leadership always makes a difference.

- ⫽ Leadership is hard to find.

- ⫽ When we do find leadership, we should cherish it, honor it, and encourage it.

Leadership makes the difference in everything, everywhere. We owe it to those who follow to provide them with the requisite mentoring.

DARE TO BE A LEADER.

SELECTED BIBLIOGRAPHY

Selections marked with ** have been cited
or referenced in the text.

** Anderson, David R., Dennis J. Sweeney, and Thomas A. Williams. *An Introduction to Management Science.* 6th ed. St. Paul, Minnesota: West Publishing Co., 1991.

** Anderson, Dean, and Linda Ackerman Anderson. *Beyond Change Management: Advanced Strategies for Today's Transformational Leaders.* San Francisco: Jossey-Bass, 2001.

** James G. Anderson. "Bureaucratic Rules: Bearers of Organizational Authority." *Educational Administration Quarterly.*

Autry, J. A. *Love and Profit: the Art of Caring Leadership.* New York: Morrow, 1991.

Agyris, Chris. *Overcoming Organizational Defenses: Facilitating Organizational Learning.* Boston: Allyn and Bacon, 1990.

Bass, Bernard. M., and Ralph M. Stogdill. *Bass and Stogdill's Handbook of Leadership: Theory, Research & Managerial Applications.* 3rd ed. New York: The Free Press, 1990.

Baron, David, and Lynette Padwa. *Moses on Management:50 Leadership Lessons from the Greatest Manager of All Time.* New York: Pocket Books, 1999.

** Bennis, Warren. "The Leader as Storyteller." *Harvard Business Review* January-February 1996: 154-159.

—. *On Becoming a Leader.* Boston: Addison Wesley, 1994.

—. *Why Leaders Can't Lead.* San Francisco: Jossey-Bass Publishers, 1989.

Bennis, Warren, and Patricia Ward Biederman. *Organizing Genius: The Secrets of Creative Collaboration.* Reading, Massachusetts: Addison-Wesley Publishing, 1997.

** Bennis, Warren, and Joan Goldsmith. *Learning to Lead: A Workbook on Becoming a Leader.* New York: Addison-Wesley, 1994.

Bennis, Warren, Gretchen M. Spreitzer, and Thomas G. Cummings, ed. *The Future of Leadership.* San Francisco: Jossey-Bass Publishers, 2001.

Blanchard, Ken, and Sheldon Bowles. *Gung Ho! Turn on the People in Any Organization.* New York: William Morrow and Co., 1997.

Blanchard, Ken, John P. Carlos, and Alan Randolph. *Empowerment Takes More Than a Minute.* San Francisco: Berrett-Koehler Publishers, 1995.

—. *The 3 Keys to Empowerment.* San Francisco: Berrett-Koehler Publishers, 1999.

** Blanchard, Ken, and Spencer Johnson. *The One Minute Manager.* New York: William Morrow and Company, 1982.

Blanchard, Ken, and Don Shula. *Everyone's a Coach.* New York: HarperBusiness Zondervan Publishing House, 1995.

Blanchard, Ken, Patricia Zigarmi, and Drea Zigarmi. *Leadership and the One Minute Manager.* New York: William Morrow & Co., 1985.

Bolman, L.G., and T. E. Deal. *Reframing Organizations: Artistry, Choice and Leadership.* San Francisco: Jossey-Bass, 1991.

** "Brave New World Meets Old World Guardian." *Daniels Alumni Review* Summer 1999, Issue 4: 1-2.

** Brodt, Audrey. "Don't You Believe It!" *Zenith Woman* Fall 2000: 17.

** Burns, James MacGregor. *Leadership.* New York: Harper & Row Publishers, 1978.

** Charan, R., and Geoffrey Colvin. "Why CEO's Fail." *Fortune* 21 June 1999:69-78.

Coles, Robert. *Lives of Moral: Leadership.* New York: Random House, 2000.

Conger, Jay, and R.N. Kanungo. *Charismatic Leadership: The Elusive Factor in Organizational Effectiveness*. San Francisco: Jossey-Bass, 1988.

** Covey, Stephen R. *Principle Centered Leadership*. New York: Simon and Schuster, 1991.

—. *The Seven Habits of Highly Effective People*. New York: Simon and Schuster, 1989.

** Deming, W. Edwards. *The New Economics for Industry, Government, Education*. Cambridge, Massachusetts: The MIT Press, 2000.

** DePree, Max. *Leadership is an Art*. New York: Dell Publishing, 1989.

—. *Leadership Jazz*. New York: Dell Publishing, 1993.

—. *Leading Without Power*. San Francisco: Jossey-Bass, 1997.

Dodson, Paul. "Author Cites Stories of Business Success." *South Ben Tribune* 26 November 1991: C5.

Dreher, Diane, et al. *The Tao of Personal Leadership*. New York: Harper Business, 1997.

** Drucker, Peter F. "The Age of Social Transformation." *The Atlantic Monthly* November 1994: 53-80.

—. *The Effective Executive*. New York: Harper Colophon, 1995.

**——. *Innovation and Entrepreneurship: Practice and Principles.* New York: Harper & Row Publishers, 1986.

**——. *Management Challenges for the 21st Century.* New York: HarperBusiness, 2001.

**——. *Post-Capitalist Society.* New York: HarperBusiness, 1994.

** Ellis, Kristine. "A Ticket to Ride." *Training* April 2001: 40-52.

Farkas, Charles M., and Phillippe De Backer. *Maximum Leadership.* New York: Henry Holt and Company, Inc., 1996.

** Farnham, Alan. "Mary Kay's Lessons in Leadership." *Fortune* 20 September 1993.

** Foster, Dick. "Victim of Highway Shooting Dies." *Rocky Mountain News* 19 March 1992: Colorado & The West: 10.

** Fowles, John. *The Magus.* New York: Dell Publishing Company, 1978.

** "From Adversity to Opportunity." Address by the Chief Executive The Honourable Tung Chee Hwa at the Legislative Council meeting on 7 October 1998.

Gardner, John. *On Leadership.* New York: Free Press, 1990.

** Getzels, Jacob W., and Egon E. Guba, "Social Behavior and the Administrative Process," *The School Review* LXV, No 4 (Winter 1957): 423-41.

** Goleman, Daniel. "Leadership That Gets Results." *Harvard Business Review* March-April 2000: 78-90.

** Goodman, Edward, and Ted Goodman. ed. *The Forbes Book of Business Quotations.* New York: Black Dog & Leventhal Publishers, 1997.

Greenleaf, Robert. *Servant Leadership: A Journey into the Nature of Legitimate Power and Greatness.* New Jersey: Paulist Press, 1983.

Hayward, Steven F. *Churchill on Leadership: Executive Success in the Face of Adversity.* California: Prima Publishing, 1997.

Heider, John, *The Tao of Leadership.* New York: Bantam, 1986.

Heifetz, Ronald. *Leadership Without Easy Answers.* Cambridge: Harvard University Press, 1994.

Helgesen, Sally. *The Female Advantage: Women's Ways of Leadership.* New York: Doubleday-Currency, 1990.

** Hersey, Paul, and Kenneth H. Blanchard. *Management of Organizational Behavior: Utilizing Human Resources.* New Jersey: Prentice-Hall, Inc., 1972.

Hesselbein, Frances, Marshall Goldsmith, and Richard Beckhard, eds. *The Leader of the Future.* San Francisco: Jossey-Bass, 1997.

Hesselbein, Frances, Marshall Goldsmith, and Iain Somerville, eds. *Leading Beyond the Walls*. San Francisco: Jossey-Bass, 1999.

Hickman, C.R. *Mind of a Manager: Soul of a Leader.* New York: Wiley, 1990.

** Huff, Darrell. *How to Lie With Statistics.* New York: W. W. Norton & Company, 1954, 1982, 1993.

** Hummel, Ralph P. *The Bureaucratic Experience.* New York: St. Martin's Press, Inc., 1977.

** Huxley, Aldous. *Brave New World.* New York: HarperCollins, 1998.

** "I Have a Dream." *Rocky Mountain News* 17 January 1994: Spotlight, 3D.

** "Ignorance is Bliss." *World Vision Today* Spring 2000: 15.

Jaworski, Joseph. *Synchronicity: The Inner Path of Leadership.* San Francisco: Berrett-Kohler, 1996.

** Jones, Julia Hughes. "Tips for Effective Leadership." *Vital Speeches* 15 January 1998: 278-281.

** Keel, Phillip. *All About Me.* New York: Broadway Books, 1998.

** Koch, John. "The Interview: Jack Galvin." *The Boston Globe* 17 January 1999: 8-9.

Kotter, John P. *Force for Change: How Leadership Differs from Management*. New York: Free Press, 1990.

—. *Leading Change*. Cambridge:Harvard Business School Publishing, 1996.

—. *What Leaders Really Do*. Cambridge:Harvard Business School Publishing, 1999.

** Kouzes, James M., and Barry Z. Posner. *Credibility*. San Francisco: Jossey-Bass, 1993.

—. *The Leadership Challenge*. San Francisco: Jossey-Bass Publishers, 1996.

Lee, Blaine. *The Power Principle: Influence with Honor*. New York: Simon and Schuster, 1997.

** Lewan, Lloyd S. "The Glass Ceiling — Another View." *Women's Business News* September 1995: 12.

** Lewan, Lloyd S., and Ron G. Billingsley. *Women in the Workplace: A Man's Perspective*. Denver: Remington Press, 1988.

** Linton, Ralph. "One Hundred Per Cent American." *The American Mercury* Vol XL, 1937: 417-419.

Loden, Marilyn. *Feminine Leadership: How to Succeed in Business Without Being One of the Boys*. New York: Times Books, 1985.

** Lopez, Isabel O. "Leadership Defined." *Colorado Business Magazine* June 1990: 89.

Lundy, James L. *Lead, Follow or Get Out of the Way: Invaluable Insights into Leadership Style*. Port Saint Lucia, Florida: Slawson Communications, Inc.,1986.

Manz, Charles C., and Henry Sims. *Super Leadership:Leading Others to Lead Themselves*. New York: Pondview Books, 1990.

Maxwell, John C. *The 21 Irrefutable Laws of Leadership: Follow Them and People Will Follow You*. Nashville: Thomas Nelson Publishers, 1998.

** McGregor, Douglas, "Conditions of Effective Leadership in Industrial Organizations," *Journal of Consulting Psychologists* 8 (1944), 56-63.

McCauley, Cynthia D. et al eds. *The Center for Creative Leadership Handbook of Leadership Development*. San Francisco: Jossey-Bass, 1998.

** Melville, Herman. *Moby Dick*. New York: The New American Library. 1961.

Myrer, Anton. *Once an Eagle*. New York: HarperCollins Publishers, 2000.

Nair, Keshavan. *A Higher Standard of Leadership: Lessons from the Life of Ghandi*. San Francisco:Berrett-Koehler, 1994.

Nanus, Burt, and Warren G. Bennis. *Leaders: Strategies for Taking Charge*. Harper Business, 1997.

Nanus, Burt. *The Leader's Edge: The Seven Keys to Leadership in a Turbulent World.* NTC Publishing Group, 1991.

Oakley, Ed, and Doug Krug, *Enlightened Leadership: Getting to the Heart of Change.* New York: Simon and Schuster, 1991.

Peters, Tom, and Nancy K Austin. *A Passion for Excellence. The Leadership Difference.* New York: Warner Books, 1985.

** Pfriem, David C. "When There is Order, There is Little to Do." *Today's HealthCare Manager* May-June 1994: 8.

Phillips, Donald. T. *The Founding Fathers on Leadership* . New York: Warner Books, 1998.

—. *Lincoln on Leadership: Executive Strategies for Tough Times.* New York: Warren Books, 1993.

** Powell, General Colin. "Career and Personal Development: 18 Lessons from a Very Successful Leader." www.littleafrica.com/career/powell. 8/22/2001.

** —. *My American Journey: An Autobiography.* New York: Random House, 1995.

** Prichett, Price. *The Employee Handbook of New World Habits for a Radically Changing World.* Dallas: Pritchett & Associates, Inc., 1994.

** —. *New Work Habits for the Next Millennium.* Dallas: Pritchett & Associates, Inc., 1999.

** Roberts, Wes. *Leadership Secrets of Attila the Hun.* New York: Warren Books, 1987.

Schwartz, Tony. *What Really Matters: Searching for Wisdom in America.* New York: Bantam, 1995.

Senge, Peter M. *The Fifth Discipline: The Art & Practice of the Learning Organization.* New York: Doubleday & Company, 1994.

Shelton, Ken, and Warren Bennis. *Beyond Counterfeit Leadership: How You Can Become a More Authentic Leader.* Provo, Utah: Executive Excellence Publishing; 1997.

** "Speed, Simplicity, Self-Confidence: An Interview with Jack Welch." *Harvard Business Review* Article No 89543.

Tichy, Noel M., and Eli Cohen. *The Leadership Engine: How Winning Companies Build Leaders at Every Level.* New York: Pondview Books, 1997.

** Teerlink, Rich. "Harley's Leadership U-Turn." *Harvard Business Review* July-August 2000: 43-48.

** "Three Days at Mickey U." *Business Month* October 1990: 24.

Tomlinson, Gerald. "Managing to Lead." *Leadership* 31 October 2000: 29.

** Tutu, Desmond. *No Future Without Forgiveness*. New York: Doubleday, 1999.

** Tzu, Lao. *Tao Te Ching*. Trans. Gia–Fu Feng and Jane English. New York: Vintage Books, 1989.

***Webster's New Universal Unabridged Dictionary*. New York: Barnes & Noble, Inc., 1996.

** Welch, Jack. *Jack: Straight from the Gut*. New York: Warren Books, Inc., 2001.

Wren, J.T. *The Leadership Companion*. New York: Free Press, 1995.

** Zaleznik, Abraham. *The Managerial Mystic: Restoring Leadership in Business*. New York: Harper & Roe, 1989.

** —. "What Makes a Leader." *Success* June 1989: 42-45.

** Zemke, Ron. "Here Come the Millennials." *Training* July 2001: 44-49.

FOR INFORMATION

For information about this book and others
by Lloyd S. Lewan, as well as information
about speaking engagements,
please write or call:

Lloyd S. Lewan
4141 East 6th Avenue
Denver, CO 80220

303-968-2221
lloyd.lewan@lewan.com